THE PROBATIVE VALUE OF DOCUMENTS IN ECCLESIASTICAL TRIALS

THE CATHOLIC UNIVERSITY OF AMERICA
CANON LAW STUDIES
No. 171

The Probative Value of Documents In Ecclesiastical Trials

(*De Fide Instrumentorum*)

AN HISTORICAL SYNOPSIS
AND COMMENTARY

BY
REV. ROBERT A. WILLETT, J.C.L.
Priest of the Archdiocese of Louisville

A DISSERTATION

Submitted to the Faculty of Canon Law of the Catholic University of America in Partial Fulfillment of the Requirements for the Degree of Doctor of Canon Law

THE CATHOLIC UNIVERSITY OF AMERICA PRESS
WASHINGTON, D. C.
1942

NIHIL OBSTAT:

Ludovicus Motry, S.T.D., J.C.D.,
Censor Deputatus.
Washingtonii, D. C. die I Julii, 1942.

IMPRIMATUR:

✠Joannes A. Floersh, D.D.,
Archiepiscopus Ludovicopolitanus.
Ludovicopoli, die III Julii, 1942.

Murray & Heister
Washington, D. C.

Printed by

Times and News Publishing Co.
Gettysburg, Pa., U. S. A.

TO
THE LOVING MEMORY OF MY
MOTHER AND FATHER

TABLE OF CONTENTS

PART II
Canonical Commentary

CHAPTER VI

CHAPTER VII

CHAPTER VIII

FOREWORD

The principle of canon 1812 that proof by documents, either public or private, is admitted in all kinds of trials, unmistakably asserts the universal use of this means of evidence in ecclesiastical procedure, whether the case deals with criminal or contentious matters.

It is apparent, however, that in many cases especially of a criminal nature documentary evidence will be lacking. But if and when this means of proof is present or can be obtained, it must be given its proper consideration in the trial. Persons who are in possession of such documents must therefore, upon a demand of the court, deliver them, but the duty of the accused is no more extensive than his obligation to testify.[1]

Documents can be regarded from a twofold viewpoint, namely, documents may constitute a contract, fact or transaction, or they may merely certify and evidence something outside of themselves. A document in the latter case is only a written testimony of an act already valid and complete without it. Such would be a case of a document's evidencing the fact of marriage, baptism, etc. The writing does not constitute the validity of such acts; it merely serves in the future to prove the act. In the former case, however, though primarily the document is a means or condition (*sine qua non*) of constituting the act, it likewise serves as a means of proof. Such is the case with betrothal contracts.[2] Whenever therefore, Canon or Civil Law requires a formal document to substantiate an act, it is demanding something more than written evidence; it is making the form of the document necessary for the validity of the act, as when Canon Law requires the signature

[1] Cf. Canon 1823, § 1: "Nemo tamen exhibere tenetur documenta, etsi communia, quae communicari nequeunt sine periculo damni ad normam can. 1755, § 2, n. 2 aut sine periculo violationis secreti servandi."

§ 2. "Attamen si qua saltem documenti particula, quam produci intersit, describi possit, et in exemplari exhiberi sine memoratis incommodis, iudex decernere potest ut eadem exhibeatur."

[2] Canon 1017, § 1.

of the bishop or pastor for the instrument constituting the betrothal, or when Civil Law requires a seal to a deed, or the signatures of three witnesses to a will. Since there is no betrothal without the signature, no will without the signatures of the witnesses and no deed without the seal, so neither the act nor any of its parts exists without the writing. Yet the very nature of such a document also offers evidence or proof of the act which it constitutes. The scope of this dissertation is confined to the consideration of documents from the viewpoint of proof.

As the Table of Contents will show, this work is divided into two general parts, with a chapter of preliminary notions and divisions preceding the first part. The aim of the first part is to trace briefly the historical development of the value of written instruments or of documents as a means of proof. Since this part is considered primarily from the standpoint of history, its presentation does not necessarily enter into the detailed discussion of each particular species of documents and of their use in practice; it rather limits itself to a brief review of the origin and the gradual development of this means of proof in so far as it had its influence on the Code of Canon Law.

The second general part is a commentary on the present law regarding documents as a means of proof, as outlined in canons 1812-1818 of the Code of Canon Law.

The author wishes to extend a sincere expression of gratitude to His Excellency, the Most Reverend John A. Floersh, Archbishop of Louisville, for the opportunity offered for advanced study in Canon Law. To the members of the Faculty of the School of Canon Law at the Catholic University of America, to the staff of the Catholic University Library, and to all others who have in any way made this work possible, the writer wishes to express his profound appreciation and gratitude.

CHAPTER I

Preliminary Notions and Divisions

ARTICLE I. NOTIONS

The title, DE FIDE INSTRUMENTORUM, introduced into the First Compilation[1] by Bernard of Pavia (+ 1213) and definitely into the Decretal Law[2] by St. Raymond of Penyafort (+ 1275), whose example was followed by all the pre-Code writers, has been retained in the Code of Canon Law.[3]

The early Romans used the term *instrumentum* in so wide a sense that it designated anything that could be used as evidence in trial.[4] With the introduction of writing as a means of proof,[5] however, the term gradually lost its general significance and was limited to designate writings alone in contrast with the other means of proof. Riccobono demonstrates the fact that the Compilers of Justinian's time freely substituted the term *instrumentum* for that of *tabula, scriptura* and *epistola.*[6]

---

[1] Cpl. I, lib. II, tit. 15.

[2] X, II, 22.

[3] Lib. IV, tit. X, cap. V, *De Probatione per Instrumenta,* art. I, *De Natura et Fide Instrumentorum.*

[4] D. (22, 4).

[5] "Probatio est ostensio rei dubiae per legitimos modos iudici facienda in causis apud ipsum iudicem controversis."—Mascardus, *Conclusiones Omnium Probationum quae in Utroque Jure Quotidie Versantur* (3 vols., Venetiis, 1593), I, q. II, n. 17. This definition is accepted and used by modern authors. Cf. Lega, *Praelectiones In Textum Iuris Canonici De Iudiciis Ecclesiasticis,* I, *De Iudiciis Ecclesiasticis Civilibus* (2. ed., Romae, 1905), n. 439; Noval, *Commentarium Codicis Iuris Canonici,* lib. IV, *De Processibus,* pars I, *De Iudiciis* (Romae, 1920), n. 439; Coronata, *Institutiones Iuris* Canonici (5 vols., Taurini: Marietti, 1928-1936), n. 1272; Roberti, *De Processibus* (2 vols., Romae: Apud Aedes Facultatis Iuridicae ed. S. Apollinaris, 1926), II, n. 324; Vermeersch-Creusen, *Epitome Iuris Canonici* (3 vols., Mechliniae: H. Dessain, Vol. I, 6. ed., 1937; Vol. II, 5. ed., 1934; Vol. III, 5. ed., 1936), III, n. 163.

[6] "Traditio Ficta,"—*Zeitschrift der Savigny Stiftung für Rechtsgeschichte, Romanistische Abteilung,* XXXIV (1913), 237.

With but few exceptions[7] the Decretals make use of the term in the restricted meeting.[8] Later the classical canonists strictly and properly defined an instrument as any writing drawn up or produced for the purpose of proving a fact.[9] It is not necessary, as this definition would lead one to believe, that in the act of drawing up the instrument the writer have the intention that it is for the purpose of proving some fact at a future time, for it is sufficient that the instrument be suited for this purpose.[10]

This species of proof is therefore preconstituted (*praeconstitutiva*). It was termed by the early canonists as *probatio probata* if the proof was derived from a public instrument, but as *probatio probanda* in case the instrument was a private writing. The same meaning is sanctioned by the Code, for a public instrument is presumed genuine[11] and true, and as such proves itself and at the same time constitutes full proof[12] of the facts related therein. This presumption is not given in favor of private writings, but their genuineness must be proved.

Furthermore, as it stands, this title *De Fide Instrumentorum* may as well refer to a writing which pertains to the substance of an act,[13] as to one which is drawn up merely to prove a fact in the

---

[7] Cf., e.g., c. 4, X, *de testibus cogendis, vel non,* II, 21.

[8] X, *de fide instrumentorum,* II, 22, *in toto.*

[9] Reiffenstuel, *Ius Canonicum Universum* (6 vols., Parisiis, 1831-1837), lib. II, tit. 22. nn. 2-4; Schmalzgrueber, *Ius Ecclesiasticum Universum* (5 vols. in 12, Romae, 1843-1845), lib. III, tit. 22, n. 1; Devoti, *Jus Canonicum Universum et Privatum* (3 vols., Romae, 1803), III, tit. 9, n. 20; Pirhing, *Ius Canonicum in V. Libros Decretalium* (5 vols., Dilingae, 1674-1678), II, 299.

[10] Wernz-Vidal, *Ius Canonicum* (7 tomes in 8 vols., Romae: Apud Aedes Universitatis Gregorianae, 1923-1938), tom. VI, *De Processibus* (1927), n. 507, p. 448, note 4; Coronata, *Institutiones,* n. 1340.

[11] Canon 1814.

[12] "Probatio plena ita definiri solet, quod illa fit, quae tantam fidem faciat, quantam ad finiendam controversiam sufficiat."—Mascardus, *Conclusiones Omnium Probationum,* I, q. IV, n. 15. Cf. Schmalzgrueber, *Ius Ecclesiasticum Universum,* lib. IV, tit. 19, n. 8; Whalen, *The Value of Testimonial Evidence in Matrimonial Procedure,* The Catholic University of America Canon Law Studies, n. 99 (Washington, D. C.: The Catholic University of America, 1935), p. 56; S. R. R., *Impedimenti ad matrimonium,* 22 ian. 1911, *coram R.P.D. Aloysio Sincero,* dec. IV, n. 7—*Decisiones,* III (1911), 35.

[13] Canons 1017, § 1; 1740, § 2; 1529.

future.[14] Consequently, in that part of the Code of Canon Law which treats *ex professo* of proof by written instruments, and to which the article *De Natura et Fide Instrumentorum* belongs,[15] there now appears the more appropriate and restricted title, *De Probatione per Instrumenta.* It is merely for a historical reason that there has been used in this title the term *instrumenta,* and not, as might logically be expected, the term *documenta.* The former term is quite generally identified in meaning with the latter, and in the pertinent canons it is the term *documenta* which is ordinarily employed.[16]

The Code in Chapter V of Title X, *De Probationibus,* speaks of instruments,[17] writings[18] and documents[19] without making any distinction. Hence it seems, at least in the portion of the Code under discussion, that these terms are to be accepted as synonymous.[20] Muniz, however, sees a difference. He teaches that a writing (*scriptura*) is a generic term, referring in any manner whatsoever to a recorded word or fact which may or may not have a relation to a trial, while instruments (*instrumenta*) are writings which are drawn up for the purpose of proving

---

[14] Generally a writing is used merely for the proving of an act. Only when the law expressly requires it is a writing necessary for its substance or validity. However, in those cases wherein the law requires a writing for the substance of the act or contract the same writing is also required for the proving of that fact or contract, and this proof cannot be supplied by witnesses, except to prove that the instrument was properly drawn up and later lost or destroyed. Cf. Coronata, *Institutiones,* n. 1339; S.R.R., *Lodonen. Incardinatio,* 9 ian. 1912, *coram R.P.D. Antonio Perathoner,* dec. 11, n. 9—*Decisiones* IV (1912), 19: "Quando autem scriptura necessaria est ad substantiam actus, necessaria quoque est, ut probati docent auctores, ad probationem actus, ita ut testes tantummodo haud sufficiant."

[15] Lib. IV, tit. X, cap. V, art. I, canons 1812-1818.

[16] Lega-Bartoccetti, *Commentarius in Iudicia Ecclesiastica* (3 vols., Romae: Anonima Libraria Cattolica Italiana, 1938-1941), II, 780.

[17] Canon 1813 § 1, n. 2.

[18] Canon 1815.

[19] Canons 1813 sq.

[20] Such is the opinion of Wernz-Vidal, *Ius Canonicum,* VI, n. 507, note 5:—"In canonibus huius capitis occurrunt voces: *instrumentum, documentum, scriptura,* quae accipiuntur ut synonima." Cf. also Coronata, *Institutiones,* n. 1340, note 2; Roberti, *De Processibus,* II, 366.

judicial acts, or which at least have been recorded for the purpose of proving facts in a trial, and, finally, documents (*documenta*) are writings furnishing proof either in or outside of court.[21] That a real distinction exists between a writing, on the one hand, and instruments and documents, on the other, can and must be readily admitted. For, taken in its generic significance, a writing includes not only instruments and documents, but also private or personal letters, annotations, etc. However, Muniz's distinction between instruments and documents, while it is a valid one, has no practical application when considered in the light of their probative value. Since the Code does not make such distinctions, and for the added reason of avoiding all ambiguity, writings, instruments and documents, unless otherwise noted,[22] will be considered as synonymous in the following pages.

ARTICLE II. DIVISIONS

An instrument or document may be either of a public or of a private character. The nature of its specific character may be determined as such either in view of its authorship or in view of the effects and consequences which by law or custom are attached to it.

A public document is a writing which relates an act that was executed by, or in the presence of, a public official acting as such, and then was properly committed to writing by the same official, or at least was signed by him. This definition, which looks to authorship as the predetermining factor for revealing the character of the instrument or document, is used by Reiffenstuel,[23] Schmalzgrueber,[24] and other leading interpreters of the pre-Code law. The present Code has not effected any change in this definition.[25] Two elements, therefore, are required—a public

---

[21] *Procedimientos Eclesiásticos* (2. ed., 3 vols., Sevilla, Lib. de Sobrino de Izquierdo, no date), III, n. 361.

[22] Cf. *infra.*

[23] *Ius Canonicum Universum,* lib. II, tit. 22, n. 7.

[24] *Ius Ecclesiasticum Universum,* lib. III, tit. 22, n. 3.

[25] Noval, *De Iudiciis,* n. 541; Wernz-Vidal, *Ius Canonicum,* VI, n. 507, p. 449; Roberti, *De Processibus,* II, n. 367; Augustine, *A Commentary on the New Code of Canon Law* (8 vols., Vol. VII, *Ecclesiastical Trials,* St. Louis: Herder, 1921), VII, 254. Hereafter cited as *Ecclesiastical Trials.*

person and the due form. A public person, strictly so called, is a notary or one who holds an office which by the designation of the public authority of a perfect society is constituted for the notarization of juridical acts.[26] Many of the modern commentators seem to have overlooked the fact that the act must be executed by or in the presence of a public official. For if this detail were not necessary, he would not be able to attest the truth of the contents as set down in the document, which attestation is required in a public instrument.[27] That he acts in his official capacity is seen: 1) when the nature of the business written is not personal but official; 2) when it contains an express statement that it is issued in the writer's official capacity; 3) when the document is countersigned by another official; 4) when use is made of the public seal of office. The use of the seal is the most common way of determining the writer's official capacity.[28]

The due form consists in the observance of the formalities or solemnities required by law or custom for a public document.[29] It is difficult to set any definite rule as to the requirements for a public document.[30] The classical canonists, under the title *De Fide Instrumentorum,* treated these solemnities at great length, prescribing all those which were introduced in Roman law as well as others which, as they asserted, had been added through custom.[31] Many of these solemnities are no longer essential today, even for documents pertaining to the substance of an act, such as the invocation of the Divine Name, the name of the reigning Pope

---

[26] Noval, *De Iudiciis,* n. 541.

[27] "Requiritur . . . ut negotio, de quo testatur, fuerit corporaliter praesens, aut partes, inter quas negotium gestum, quasi de novo omnia repetant."—*De Angelis Praelectiones Juris Canonici* (4 vols., Romae, 1877-1887), IV, lib. II, tit. 22, art. 1.

[28] Noval, *De Iudiciis,* n. 545.

[29] Schmalzgrueber, *Ius Ecclesiasticum Universum,* lib. III, tit. 22, n. 43.

[30] "Difficile admodum est in concordiam reducere auctores antiquos inter se et multo magis cum modernis . . . in praecipua hac prima divisione (publicum, privatum) et conditionibus requisitis ad illam appellationem."—Wernz-Vidal, *Ius Canonicum,* VI, n. 507, p. 449, note 6.

[31] Reiffenstuel, *Ius Canonicum Universum,* lib. II, tit. 22, nn. 18 sq.; Schmalzgrueber, *Ius Ecclesiasticum Universum,* lib. III, tit. 22, nn. 12 sq.; De Angelis, *Praelectiones Juris Canonici,* IX, pars II, lib. II, tit. 22, art. 1.

or civil ruler, etc. In listing the solemnities required for a public document, Justinian made mention of the Divine Name (auctore deo).[32] This invocation, however, had no legal significance. It was rather a praiseworthy practice of Christian piety, dedicating a legal instrument, as any other work, to the service of God.[33] Gudelinus[34] concurs in this opinion by stating that the invocation of the Divine Name does not pertain exclusively to documents but equally to other affairs; that consequently, if it is added, it must be considered merely as a pious act, and that its omission in no way changes or vitiates the value of the instrument. Although canon 1874, § 1, directs that every sentence should begin with an invocation of the Divine Name,[35] Coronata states that this solemnity seems not to be necessary for validity.[36] Furthermore, the Divine Invocation is not included in canon 1894 where the requirements whose omission vitiates a sentence by curable nullity are enumerated. After listing the solemnities enumerated by the classical canonists, Ferraris remarks:

> Supradictae solemnitates, quamvis non omnes de rigore iuris requirantur ad essentiam seu substantiam instrumenti publici, solent tamen omnes secundum receptam consuetudinem adhiberi, ita ut, si aliqua omittantur, tale instrumentum de fraude et falsitate suspectum reddatur; unde servandae sunt secundum cuiuslibet provinciae probatam consuetudinem.[37]

If not all the external solemnities enumerated by the classical canonists are required today, even for the documents which are necessary for the substance of an act, *a fortiori* not all are required for documents pertaining merely to the proving of an

---

[32] Nov. 47, 1.

[33] Cooper, *Institutes of Justinian* (3. ed., New York, 1852), p. 401.

[34] *Commentariorum de Iure Novissimo Libri Sex* (Florentiae, 1839), p. 179.

[35] "Sententia ferri debet, divino Nomine ab initio semper invocato."

[36] "Haec sollemnitas, ut videtur, ad valorem non esse necessaria."—*Institutiones*, n. 1404.

[37] *Prompta Bibliotheca Canonica, Iuridica, Moralis, Theologica, nec non Ascetica, Polemica, Rubricistica, Historica* (9 vols., Romae, 1885-1899), VII, V, "Scriptura seu Instrumentum," n. 71.

act. For the purpose of these solemnities is to prevent forgery and to aid the judge in deciding whether the document in question is or is not genuine. Consequently, they are to be considered as a means to an end rather than as an end in themselves.

Thus custom has modified the requirements, so that the official style in the present law requires the following solemnities for a public document: 1) the signature of a suited person appointed for drawing up the act in question, namely, that of a notary or of some other public person recognized as such by the Code;[38] 2) his seal[39] or at least the seal of his office, for instance, the diocesan or episcopal, the parish or monastery seal; 3) the date and place of issuance.[40] However, the essential element for a public document, of any other public person appointed for this purpose. The other conditions noted in the common law seem not to be necessary for validity.

Public instruments are subdivided into *protocols* and *transcripts.*

During the course of time the meaning of these terms has somewhat changed. Formerly a protocol was a succinct or rough draft briefly relating the minutes of a meeting or transaction which was later written out fully with the required formalities.[42] At the present time, however, the custom of taking the original from the protocol is not generally observed; and a protocol is understood to be a register in which are marked, by brief indications, the charts or letters sent or received by any office or physical or moral person. In a protocol should be noted the date, place, person to whom the document was sent and the object concerning which it treats. The

---

[38] E.g., ordinaries, or also pastors in regard to parochial registers. Cf. canon 1813.

[39] "Sigillum idest parvum signum est imago cera aut alia materia impressa ad aliquid signandum seu ab aliis rebus modo certo distinguendum. Potest esse authenticum et non authenticum, publicum aut privatum. Multa de his disputant antiqui canonistae."—Reiffenstuel, *Ius Canonicum Universum,* lib. II, tit. 22 nn. 70-101.

[40] Coronata, *Institutiones,* n. 1341; Augustine, *Ecclesiastical Trials,* p. 254.

according to Coronata,[41] seems to be the signature of a notary or

[41] *Loc. cit.*

[42] Reiffenstuel, *Ius Canonicum Universum,* lib. II, tit. 22, nn. 34 sq.; Lega, *De Iudiciis Ecclesiasticis Civilibus,* I, n. 452.

documents in the protocol or register should, furthermore, be numbered according to some logical and recognized system.[43] It is to be understood that, in order to be classed as a public document, the protocol must be kept by a public person or at least under his supervision.

Formerly a transcript (*transumptum*) was any original document which had been fully written out with the formalities, in contradistinction to the protocol.[44] Now the term is used for an examplar or copy of the original writing.[45] Wherefore, these terms, as understood by the pre-Code writers, are practical only when there is question of a document of the pre-Code law appearing in the form of a protocol or transcript.

A private instrument is one which is drawn up either by a private person in any form, or by a public person who does not act in his official capacity or who has omitted some formality which is required for making the instrument a public one.[46] Thus a bishop, pastor or notary may write out a receipt (*apocha*), draw up a written bilateral contract (*syngrapha*), and draft a letter or will, and thus constitute documents of an entirely private character.[47] Numbered also among the private instruments which may be utilized as means of proof are those writings which bear no signature, such as the account books of heads of families, of merchants, of brokers, of teachers, of guardians, of administrators, etc., and in general all annotations of a non-official character.[48]

Public instruments when considered from the view-point of their authorship are likewise divided into ecclesiastical and civil instruments in relative dependence upon the fact that they were drawn up by persons who were ecclesiastics or civilians.

---

[43] Ferretti, *I piccoli archivi ecclesiastici e le piccole biblioteche, riordinate secondo il codice di diritto can. e i principali sinodi diocesani* (Roma, 1918), p. 18.

[44] Cf. authors cited above.

[45] Canons 2054-2056; Coronata, *Institutiones*, n. 1340; Roberti, *De Processibus*, II, 368.

[46] Augustine, *Ecclesiastical Trials*, p. 254; Lega-Bartoccetti, *Commentarius*, II, 781.

[47] Canon 1813, § 3.

[48] Lega-Bartoccetti, *Commentarius*, II, 782.

Private instruments, when considered from the view-point of their legal form and of the effects attached to them by law or custom, are divided into authentic and non-authentic (simply private) instruments. It is to be noted that an original public instrument is by its very nature necessarily authentic and thereby does not admit such a division. The term authentic has been variously explained by different authors. The classical canonists, following the doctrine of the Decretal Law,[49] understood by the term "authentic" a private writing, either in original or in copy, fortified or strengthened by the signature of witnesses or by a seal, or recognized and approved in any other legitimate manner.[50] But they were not of one mind as to what requirements were necessary for this recognition and approval.[51]

---

[49] C. 2, X, *de fide instrumentorum,* II, 22.

[50] Reiffenstuel, *Ius Canonicum Universum,* lib. II, tit. 22, n. 14; Schmalzgrueber, *Ius Ecclesiasticum Universum,* lib. III, tit. 22, n. 36.

[51] Roberti in summarizing their teaching states: "Authentica dicebatur, 'scriptura privata quidem, testium tamen subscriptione aut sigillo eoque recognito et adprobato aut alio legitimo modo munita.' Ita Schmalzgrueber, L. III, tit. XXII, n. 36; a quo sequentes scripturae authenticae considerabantur: a) acta publica et iudicialia; b) scripturae ex archivo publico depromptae; c) scripturae privatae aliquo sigillo Principis, Episcopi, civitatis, universitatis vel communitatis ius sigilli habentis, munitae; d) scripturae privatae trium aut saltem duorum testium adhuc viventium et suam manum recognoscentium subscriptione corroboratae; e) matriculae et libri censuales; f) libri officialium publicorum, parochiales, baptizatorum, nuptorum, defunctorum; libri collegiorum, opificum, etc.; g) scripturae secundum morem et consuetudinem religionis confectae quae vim authenticarum obtinuerunt quoad omnes longo tempore et usu. At plures doctores cum Durante (lib. II, part. 2 h.t. Nunc dicendum n. 2) publicis instrumentis accensebant, praeter notarilia, acta iudicialia, instrumenta subscripta a tribus testibus nec non producta ex archivo publico. Gross (o.c., II, p. 45) contra negabat documenta servata in archivo publico posse publicis documentis aequiparari, non obstante c. 13, X, II, 19, contendens nihil in Decretalibus inveniri pro assertionibus veterum canonistarum; cfr. c. I, C. XXX q. 1; 28, X, II, 20; 2, X, II, 22; 13, X, II, 26. Cfr. Reiffenstuel, lib. II, tit. 22, n. 143 ss.; Santi, lib. II, tit. XXII, n. 3 ss.; Sebastianelli, o.c., p. 170, 171. Ex enumeratis documentis, hodie publica habentur quae ponuntur sub litteris a), et ex parte sub littera f); reliqua sunt privata; sed possunt recognosci."—*De Processibus,* II, n. 367, p. 95, note 1.

Since these writings as means of proof were the equivalent of public instruments, the terms "authentic" and "public" were employed synonymously in that respect. By way of differentiation, however, the word "public" was referred to a writing which was drawn up by a notary, and the word "authentic" was attributed to a writing which of itself gave proof (*ex se fidem fecit*) in view of the fact that it carried the stamp of a public seal, for example, that of a bishop or of a secular prince, or that it was in some other equivalent manner duly authenticated. Under such conditions of proper authentication no further supporting evidence was required to lend cogency to these private instruments as means of proof.[52]

Among the modern canonists some consider "authentic" synonymous with "genuine."[53] According to Cappello "authentic" is synonymous with "original." But he states that a copy can be authenticated by the declaration of a person in public authority.[54] Noval restricts the term "authentic" to copies which have been made by public persons, and thereby furnish assurance of their concordance with the originals.[55] It is apparent, therefore, that there is no agreement either among the ancient or modern authors as to the exact use of this term. However, the terminology of the Code indicates how this term "authentic" is now to be accepted and used.

Where documents are treated *ex professo* the Code does not speak properly of authentic instruments, but rather of acts drawn up in authentic form, of authentic attestations, of authentic copies

---

[52] Cf. Reiffenstuel, *Ius Canonicum Universum,* lib. II, tit. 22, n. 14: "Etsi inter instrumentum publicum et authenticum possit notari aliqua differentia, in effectu tamen parvum interest, ac frequenter publica et authentica instrumenta sumuntur pro synonymis."

[53] Maroto, *Institutiones Iuris Canonici ad Normam Novi Codicis* (2 vols., Matriti, 1919-1921), I, n. 36. Eichmann, *Das Prozeszrecht des Codex Iuris Canonici* (Paderborn: Ferdinand Schöningh, 1921), p. 156; Wernz-Vidal, *Ius Canonicum,* VI, n. 507, III; Beste, *Introductio in Codicem* (Collegeville, Minn.: St. John's Abbey Press, 1938), p. 185.

[54] *Summa Iuris Canonici* (3 vols., Vol. III, Romae: Apud Gregorianum, 1936), III, n. 278. Also Vermeersch-Creusen, *Epitome Iuris Canonici,* III, n. 199.

[55] *De Iudiciis,* n. 541, p. 366.

and of documents in the authentic form.[56] From this fact it is clear that the Code, when it uses this term in relation to documents,[57] refers to the external form of the instruments or to the marks or solemnities through which the intrinsic value of these documents may be determined.[58] These marks or solemnities are always required for a public instrument, but they may or may not be used in attestations and copies taken from public documents as well as in private writings.

As the authentication does not change the intrinsic nature of a document,[59] but rather leads to an assured knowledge of its true nature, the Code places authentic attestations and copies of public documents in the list of public instruments.[60]

The practical question then remains: What is to be understood by an authentic and non-authentic private document? An authentic private document is a writing, indeed private by its very nature, but whose genuineness of authorship is assured by some means recognized by law or custom, e.g., by the signature of a

[56] Cf. canons 1813, § 1 nn. 1, 4; 1819; 1820.

[57] In other matters it must be admitted that even the Code considers "authentic" synonymous with "genuine." Cf. canons 1284; 1285, § 1. "Authentic" has still a different meaning in canon 17. Authentic interpretation under the terminology of canon 17, § 2, means interpretation which has the force of law or is law in its own right.—Schmidt, *The Principles of Authentic Interpretation in Canon 17 of the Code of Canon Law* (The Catholic University of America Canon Law Studies, n. 141, Washington, D. C.: The Catholic University of America Press, 1941), p. 109.

[58] "Genuina censentur quippe integre seu omnibus in suis partibus aestimantur confecta ab eo cui tamquam auctori attribuuntur; id est vel parocho vel notario aut cancellario cui illa scripta attestationes et relationes attribuuntur ex forma extrinseca et legitima unde sunt confecta et asservata. Inde *genuinitas distinguitur* ab *authenticitate,* quippe authenticitas in subiecta materia canonum est attestatio facta a persona competente quod certa scriptura est illius cui attribuitur, dum *genuinitas* latius patet et comprehendit nedum scripturae authenticitatem sed veritatem eorum quae in scriptura referuntur. Unde authenticitas magis pertinet ad veritatem seu qualitatem extrinsecam; genuinitas magis ad *intrinsecam.*"—Lega-Bartoccetti, *Commentarius,* II, 791.

[59] Roberti, *De Processibus,* II, n. 372, p. 101, note 1: "Hodie authenticationes a notariis peractae ipsae sunt publicae, sed naturam documenti privati non mutant."

[60] E.g., canon 1813, § 1, nn. 1, 4.

notary or two witnesses who are capable of testifying in court, by the affixing of a public seal, by its having been preserved in a public archive, by a judicial recognition, etc.[61] If the instrument does not bear any of these marks of authenticity it remains in the class of simple private documents. From this observation it is evident that a private document can be genuine the while it remains non-authentic.

When measured and evaluated according to the standards of truthfulness, integrity and legal efficacy, an instrument, whether public or private, is called genuine when its author is he to whom it is attributed; it is called integral when it is unchanged; it is called legitimate when it is drawn up in due form. Conversely, when an instrument is not genuine it is apocryphal; when it contains erasures, corrections or interpolations it is mutilated or defective; when it is drawn up by an unauthorized person, or concerning a proscribed object matter, or minus the solemnities and formalities essential for its legal efficacy, it is illegitimate.[62]

---

[61] Reiffenstuel, *Ius Canonicum Universum*, lib. II, tit. 22, nn. 142 sq.; Augustine, *Ecclesiastical Trials*, p. 255; Muniz, *Procedimientos Eclesiásticos*, III, n. 370, p. 303, note 1.

[62] Noval, *De Iudiciis*, n. 541; Cappello, *Summa Iuris Canonici*, III, n. 278; Lega-Bartoccetti, *Commentarius*, II, 782.

PART ONE

Historical Synopsis

CHAPTER II

Documentary Evidence in Roman Law

No system of law or any of its component parts appears suddenly in its fully developed form. It is rather the gradual crystallization of custom and the solution of arising contingencies. This is particularly true of the topic under discussion—proof by documents.

The oral word is older than the written word. Similarly oral testimony is older, in the legal order, than that furnished by writings. In ancient times verbal testimony was practically the only means of proof. However, in company with the art of writing came the custom of transcribing into written form legal transactions and court proceedings for the purpose of using them as proof in the future.

ARTICLE I. THE CLASSICAL PERIOD

The Classical period of Roman law is characterized by the theory of free-proof. The judge had great liberty in appraising the value of the proofs offered.[1] He acted on the principle of hearing all evidence and then drawing his own conclusion on the merits of each species of proof offered. The contesting parties were likewise legally free to furnish any means of proof they were able to produce. Both documents and the statements of witnesses were, in principle, equally suited for the purpose. Constantine expressed this truth by way of law in the year 317.[2] In practice, however, documentary evidence was seldom used. The reason is to be found in the fact that it was not the custom at that time to draw up contracts in writing. Furthermore, the writings of the

[1] Costa, *Profilo Storico del Processo Civile Romano* (Romae, 1918), p. 164.

[2] C. (4, 21) 15: "In exercendis litibus eandem vim obtinent tam fides instrumentorum quam depositiones testium."

Romans, before and at the time under consideration, being divested of all the formalities which might have assured their genuineness and thus in turn might have gained probative value, had no particular place in law.[3]

With attention to these reflections, one must conclude that writings in the Roman juridical world during that early period did not enjoy any privileged importance as a means of proof. In fact, Cicero in his *Pro Archia* wrote that a reliable witness was preferable to a document.[4]

ARTICLE II. THE BYZANTINE INFLUENCE IN THE POST-CLASSICAL PERIOD

Documents as a means of proof increased in use and importance under Byzantine influence. Simultaneously the depositions of witnesses as a means of proof decreased in the same degree. Constantine, who at Rome a few years previously (317) had set up the principle of perfect equality between written instruments and the oral testimony of witnesses as a potential means for obtaining proof,[5] later, in the year 334 at Naissus, in Upper Moesia, imposed limitations and enacted prohibitions regarding the admissibility of witnesses. He directed that witnesses should not be permitted to testify before they had been sworn, and that the preference should be given to those who were of honorable reputation.[6]

The complete change in favor of proof by documents came at the beginning of the reign of Justinian. Through his legislation the liberty which formerly was granted in the matter of establishing proof, and which was so prevalent in the classical period, was

---

[3] Riccobono, "Traditio Ficta,"—*Zeitschrift der Savigny-Stiftung für Rechtsgeschichte, Romanistische Abteilung,* XXXIV (1913), 232:—"Riemptio di lettere nude, che non hanno per se vita e vigore."

[4] Cicero, *Pro Archia,* 4, 8:— ". . . est ridiculum . . . cum habeas amplissimi viri religionem, integerrimi municipii iusiurandum fidemque, ea quae depravari nullo modo possunt repudiare, tabulas quas idem dicis solere corrumpi desiderare."

[5] C. (4, 21) 15.

[6] C. (4, 20) 9. For other restrictions cf. C. (4, 20) *in toto.*

restricted. Written proof now became as a rule the preeminent means and in many cases the exclusive agency.[7]

Riccobono, in his article *Traditio Ficta,* gives an extensive and lucid demonstration of the change effected by Justinian. He cites numerous examples to show that the Compilers of Justinian's Code attempted, by their interpolations, to fit the new law to the old, in accordance with the new concept of proof. In most instances the interpolations entirely changed the meaning of former rescripts, while in others, due to the carelessness of the Compilers, they made rescripts contradictory. Having given many examples evidencing these facts, Riccobono remarks: "Justinian, as we have seen, immediately at the beginning of the Codification manifests his full aversion for the proofs by means of witnesses. Therefore, the disfavor for this means of proof, which the Romans had always considered first in importance, had run its course and was firmly established in law."[8]

ARTICLE III. THE PROBATIVE VALUE OF DOCUMENTS

With Justinian's preference for documents as a means of proof the necessity arose of adding certain solemnities to documents to give them a public character and thus assure their genuineness and protect them from the danger of forgery.[9]

Greater weight was attached to all public records and properly authenticated documents duly executed by, or in the presence of, the officials charged with that duty, than to others of any description. A last will was considered a public document by the Roman jurisconsults.

A private instrument, to be legal and to have probative value, was required to be sworn to and signed by three witnesses. If

---

[7] C. (4, 20) 1:—"Contra scriptum testimonium non scriptum non profertur." Costa, *loc. cit.*

[8] *Art. cit.,* p. 245.

[9] Nov. 44, requirements of notaries; Nov. 73, witnesses; Nov. 47, external solemnities. Cf. Cooper, *Institutes of Justinian,* p. 401; Gudelimus, *Commentariorum de Jure Novissimo Libri Sex,* p. 179 sq.; Stephanus, *Commentarius in Novellas Justiniani Imperatoris* (Florentiae, 1843), p. 322 sq.

they, or any of them, were dead, their signatures could be proved to be genuine if by way of comparison with other signatures of whose genuineness there was no doubt a true and uniform likeness was discernible among all of these signatures. A personal document which was of such great age that any witnesses thereto had to be presumed in the course of nature to be no longer living could also be employed as a means of proof if no way remained for the authentication of such a document's genuineness. When a document was lost or destroyed, then no evidence concerning its contents could be given, unless its absence or non-existence was satisfactorily established under oath.

Copies of documents were admissible if their accuracy could be satisfactorily established, provided that proof was adduced that the originals were not available.[10]

---

[10] *The Civil Law as Translated by S. B. Scott* (17 vols., Cincinnati, Ohio: The Central Trust Company, 1932), XIII, 48, note 1; *Bethman-Hollweg, Der Römische Civil-process* (5 vols., Bonn, 1864-1870), II, 601 sq.

CHAPTER III

DOCUMENTARY EVIDENCE IN THE EARLY MIDDLE AGES

ARTICLE I. THE VISIGOTHIC CODE

For more than a century after their conquest of the West the Goths preserved their ancient habits and customs. During this period the victorious Goths based their laws upon these customs and upon oral tradition. But the environment of Roman society, and to a greater degree the influence of the Church's legal system, which itself contained many Roman elements, made a strong impression on the converted Goths. As a result, the passing of time noted a strong tendency towards the Romanization of Gothic laws. Yet the law did not become entirely Roman, for the kingdom remained Gothic and many of their old laws and customs were never abrogated but found their way into written Codes.

The first codification, only part of which is extant, was written by Euric, at Arles, in the latter half of the fifth century. The purpose of this Code was to govern the legal relations between Goths and Romans. The Romans, therefore, were affected by this law only in their relations with the Goths; otherwise they were permitted to live according to their own law.[1]

The old Roman law did not, however, prove practicable for all the needs of the Romans who were subject to the Gothic kingdom. To meet this contingency Alaric II, son and successor of Euric, ordered a revision of their Code. This work was compiled mainly from the Codes of pre-Justinian law, and was promulgated by Alaric in the year 506. Among other names it is ordinarily referred to as the *Breviarium Alaricianum.*[2]

---

[1] Ziegler, *Church and State in Visigothic Spain* (Washington, D. C.: The Catholic University of America, 1930), p. 59.

[2] Ziegler, *op. cit.*, p. 59.

The *Breviarium* remained in force, as the Code under which the Romans in the Visigothic kingdom lived, until Receswinth in the year 654, using the compilations of both Euric and Alaric as his sources, introduced a single and unified Code for all his subjects, known as the *Forum Judicum* or the Visigothic Code.[3]

From what has been stated above it is evident that Roman law played no minor part in the compilation of the Visigothic Code. Realizing the superiority of the Roman law, the Goths made much of it their own, thus substituting written documents for many of their ceremonial contracts.[4] "The rules, 'observes Scott,' relating to the execution, attestation and proof of wills and other legal documents, contained in the *Forum Judicum* (Visigothic Code) were, for the most part, derived from the Codes of Theodosius and Justinian."[5] Scott further states that a great part of the second book of this Code, which treats of witnesses and documents, was borrowed from the Roman jurisprudence.[6]

For the greater part the details of the procedure of the Visigothic tribunals are shrouded in obscurity, yet it can be gathered from a study of the Code that they had their summonses and other writs of various kinds, their pleadings, arguments, depositions, appraisements and judicial opinions both oral and written.[7] This much is certain, that their proof was procured by rational and material means. Both documentary evidence and the testimony of witnesses were freely employed.[8] A *lex antiqua*[9] ordered that the judge should first interrogate the witnesses and

---

[3] *Loc. cit.* Cf. also Scott, *The Visigothic Code* (*Forum Judicum*), translated from the original Latin (Boston, 1910), p. XXIX. This translation is defective in many places.

[4] Ziegler, *op. cit.*, p. 58.

[5] *Op. cit.*, p. 73. Cf. also Ziegler, *op. cit.*, p. 75.

[6] *Loc. cit.* Cf. also Ziegler, *op. cit.*, p. 76.

[7] Scott, *op. cit.*, p. XXXVI.

[8] Cf. e.g., *Leges Visigothorum*, II, 5, *in toto*, et III, 6, 2, in *Monumenta Germaniae Historica, Legum Sectio I, Leges Nationum Germanicarum*, Tom. I (ed. Karolus Zeumer, Hannoverae et Lipsiae 1902), 106-120 et 167. This collection is henceforth cited as *MGH*, and the section as *Leges Nat. Germ.*

[9] *Codicis Euriciani Leges ex Lege Baiuvariorum Restitutae*, 9 (L. Bai. 9, 17). Cf. *MGH, Legum Sectio I, Leges Nat. Germ.*, I, 20, note 1.

then examine the documents. Recourse to oaths was to be had only when all attempts to obtain reasonable proofs had failed.[10]

King Chindaswinth (elected 642) published a law enumerating the documents which were to be considered as valid in law for establishing full proof. "All documents," the law reads, "in which the day and year are clearly expressed and which are confirmed by the seals or signatures of the parties, or of witnesses, shall be deemed valid. Such documents, also, as any person on account of sickness was unable to sign, but had requested witnesses to affix their signature thereto in his presence, shall be equally valid, and also, where any one is requested to affix his seal or signature to a document, instead of the party himself, it shall be valid only under the condition that, if the maker of said document should recover from his illness, and should desire that that which has been thus attested be also irrevocably established, he have it confirmed by his own signature.

If a testator should die after making a will attested by another, as aforesaid, he who was called as witness shall see that the will is proved by him within six months, as provided by another law."[11] The law referred to here demanded a will made in these circumstances to be proved within six months, either in the presence of a priest or of witnesses.[12]

Another law provided that a witness should not sign a document before reading it or having heard it read. And if he presumed to do so, and then attempted to testify concerning what he had done negligently, his evidence was not to be accepted, and the document was to be considered void, since the authenticity of the document was not established in a legal manner.[13]

---

[10] *Leg. Vis.*, II, 1, 23, in *MGH, Legum Sectio I, Leges Nat. Germ.*, I, 70.

[11] *Leg. Vis.*, II, 5, 1 et 2, in *MGH., Legum Sectio I, Leges Nat. Germ.*, I, 106-107. The translation of this law is adapted to that of Scott, *The Visigothic Code*, p. 64. The present writer found it necessary to make some changes in this translation where it was evidently incorrect and gave an entirely different meaning to the original law, e.g., Scott translated the phrase "Scripture, que diem et annum habuerint evidenter expressum" as "all documents which have been drawn up for a year and a day."

[12] *Leg. Vis.*, II, 5, 14, in *MGH., Legum Sectio I, Leges Nat. Germ.*, I, 114.

[13] *Leg. Vis.*, II, 5, 3, in *MGH., Legum Sectio I, Leges Nat. Germ.*, I, 107.

The permanent value of a document was assured by a law of the same King Chindaswinth, which permitted and demanded that, in case the one who made the document and the witnesses thereto were dead, its genuineness should be proved by comparison of writings. "Documents of every description," the law states, "where he who made them and the witnesses to the same are dead, and in which the signature of the former and the attestation of the witnesses appear, when brought into court to be verified, may be proved by comparison of their seals and signatures with those of other documents; and the proof shall be sufficient in this investigation, if the seals and signatures of three or four other documents, when introduced, shall be evidently those of the parties in question. But, if the documents aforesaid shall not have been published within the time prescribed by law,[14] they shall be invalid."[15]

It was the right and duty of the bishop and the judge to decide whether or not the writings were identical in character.[16] The important rôle the bishops played in the evaluation of documents is very forcefully demonstrated in one instance wherein the ascent of a king to his throne depended on the judgment of the bishops, assembled in the XII Council of Toledo (681), as to the genuineness of the documents proposed.[17]

ARTICLE II. THE GERMANIC LAW

The oldest Germanic Law did not utilize documents and consequently could not allow for proof by means of written instruments. Here again the Roman influence was felt, for it was not until the Germans came into contact with Roman legal culture that they became aware of documents and began to appraise their value legally.[18]

---

[14] Within six months. Cf. *Leg. Vis.*, II, 5, 1, in *MGH., Legum Section I, Leges Nat. Germ.*, I, 106.

[15] *Leg. Vis.*, II, 5, 15, in *MGH., Legum Sectio I, Leges Nat. Germ.*, I, 113. Translation adapted to that of Scott, *The Visigothic Code*, p. 69.

[16] *Leg. Vis.*, II, 5, 16, in *MGH., Legum Sectio I, Leges Nat. Germ.*, I, 115.

[17] Ziegler, *op. cit.*, p. 114.

[18] Bresslau, *Handbuch der Urkendenlehre für Deutschland und Italien* (2 vols., Leipzig, 1889), I, 476. The second edition (1912) of this work was not available to the present writer.

The Alemannic folk law, as taken from an old MSS which, according to Brunner, dates from the first decade of the eighth century,[19] made use of documents (*cartae*) extensively. The only requisites for the legal value of such documents seem to have been, at first, that they be signed by witnesses and that they be dated.[20] Since no prescriptions are given regarding the writer of a document, the existence of public notaries can not be assumed in the *Lex Alamannorum*. The law did, however, specify that any and all transfer of ecclesiastical property to a layman must be made in writing duly witnessed. This necessitated the fact that the one acquiring such a piece of property be able to produce documentary evidence to this effect. Failing to do so, he lost all claim to possession.[21] In all other business transactions it was left to the free choice of the parties whether they were to be made by means of documents or otherwise.

Nothing was expressly stated regarding the requirements for a document to be accepted as valid in court trials; still it can be gathered that full efficacy as proof was attributed to any document in court only in case the document was not contested (*schelte*). For, in the event that the document was contested, both the one producing the said instrument and the witnesses to it were permitted to take an oath regarding the genuineness of the facts contained therein. Settlement was in favor of the possessor of the document after such an oath had been taken. No such solemn appeal to God was permitted to the opponent.[22]

The Bavarian law had the same provisions as the *Lex Alamannorum* regarding the transfer of real estate by means of a document adding, however, details as to the manner of executing the document. It provided that the deponent testify to the transfer in his own hand, and that the witnesses lay their hands on the document and, further, that their names be designated therein.[23]

[19] *Deutsche Rechtsgeschichte* (2 vols., Leipzig, 1906-1928), I, 308 sq.

[20] *Lex Alamannorum*, 5, 1, in *MGH., Leges* (5 vols., I-IV ed. Georgius Henricus Pertz, V, ed. Pertz-Waitz-Brunner, Hannoverae, 1835-1863), III, 92.

[21] *Lex Alamannorum*, 5, 18, in *MGH., Leges*, III, 95.

[22] *Lex Alamannorum*, 5, 1, in *MGH., Leges*, III, 92.

[23] *Lex Baiuwariorum*, I, 1, in *MGH., Leges*, III, 269.

It is also more specific than the *Lex Alamannorum* in emphasizing the unconditional legal validity of all commercial deals fortified by documents provided that the instrument bore a manifest expression of the year and day it was drawn up.[24]

The Bavarian law had no express provision for the trial procedure in case a document was challenged. Bresslau[25] surmises that it was the same as the Alemannic, namely, that the proponent of the instrument and its witnesses were admitted to oath. He gives weight to his assumption by calling attention to a chronicle narrating a trial of the year 829, in which a document involving a gift for the town of Freising was challenged. The possessor of the property under dispute, although in possession, was not admitted to oath after the presentation of the document.

According to Bresslau,[26] our whole knowledge of Salic legal forms in trials in which documents were employed is based on an anonymous Italian writer of a later date. The time of his life (probably the middle of the ninth century) and his credibility as a historical witness are not beyond all question. According to this Italian writer the attestation by seven witnesses was indeed required, but it also sufficed, to give a document the value of full proof, provided that the document was not contested. This writer also reveals the fact that if a document was contested (*falsam adclamare*), its proponent with twelve others swore to the genuineness of the instrument. The accuser (opponent) was not admitted to oath. However, if the accuser did not acquiesce, he had to proceed immediately before the tribunal to the act of solemn rejection. Immediately after the proponent's protestation of the genuineness of the document the opponent pierced the instrument which he termed false. Its possessor again declared its genuineness, whereupon the opponent and forty-nine aides were admitted to oath, seven against each of the seven documentary witnesses. By the taking of this oath the spuriousness of the

---

[24] "Pacta vel placita, quae per scriptura quacumque facta sunt . . . , dummodo in his dies et annus sit evidenter expressus, inmutare nulla ratione permittimus."—*Lex Baiuwariorum,* 16, 16, in *MGH., Leges,* III, 324.

[25] *Handbuch,* I, 482.

[26] *Op. cit.,* p. 481.

document was proved, provided that the proponent of the document did not demand a judicial duel to be fought to decide the contest. From the above, if it be worthy of credence, it is clear that when a document was attacked it no longer furnished an independent means of proof. But it did give its proponent an advantage in the trial.

In his *History of the Franks* St. Gregory of Tours (+ 594) gives many examples which demonstrate the use of royal documents among the Ribuarians. Many of these documents refer directly to ecclesiastical matters.[27] The *Lex Ribuaria* contains several important and comprehensive provisions on the evidential value of such documents. The most important one is that the judicial challenging of a royal document was admitted only when the opponent could quote as supporting his side a royal document to the contrary. If he had no such royal document, that is, if he opposed such a *testamentum regium absque contrario testamento,* he had to pay the penalty with his life.[28] The one guilty of such an act, however, was permitted to redeem his life by the payment of two hundred (200) *solidi.*[29]

In forbidding the challenging of a royal document only *absque contrario testamento,* the Ribuarian law provided for the case of a conflict between two royal documents. Neither was to be considered void, but the older was preferred and the disputed object was divided, two-thirds being awarded to the possessor of the older document, the remaining third to his opponent.[30] Bresslau[31] doubts that this provision was common to all the Franks. Whether or not this was the case, the later legislation of the Carlovingians did not recognize this principle. It was in the Edict of 614 that Chlotar II ordered the more recent royal document which was contrary to the earlier one to be considered as void, unless the

---

[27] *History of the Franks by Gregory of Tours,* translated with an introduction by O. M. Dalton (2 vols., Oxford, 1927), 4, 46; 6, 16; 6, 46; 7, 31; 8, 22; 10, 19.

[28] *Lex Ribuaria,* 60, 6, in *MGH., Leges,* V, 252.

[29] *Lex Ribuaria,* 57, 3, in *MGH., Leges,* V, 242.

[30] *Lex Ribuaria,* 60, 7, in *MGH., Leges,* V, 252.

[31] *Handbuch der Urkundenlehre für Deutschland und Italien,* I, 484.

more recent instrument expressly mentioned and abrogated the contrary provision of the earlier document. In this case the later document was valid, the older null.[32]

Thus far it has been seen that the law gave a document for private transactions certain preference in trial. But with the institution of public notaries these documents obtained a greater and lasting value for the establishing of judicial proof. Up to about the seventh century anyone who so desired could write his own documents, or he was permitted to employ anyone he wished to do it for him. However, in the first half of the seventh century public notaries were instituted.[33] These notaries, whose documents were accorded certain privileges in law in the process of trials, dated apparently from the time of King Dagobert I. They were generally known as *notarii* or *amanuenses* in the Salic, but as *cancellarii* in the Ribuarian and Alemannic provinces.[34] Bresslau states that they were all clerics, as the laity of Germany at that time, with but few exceptions, did not have sufficient education for the position of notary.[35]

That the documents drawn up or merely signed by these notaries gave full and independent proof, without oath or further contest, is evidenced in the Ribuarian Code.[36] It was sufficient for the notary to acknowledge his signature in order to insure the genuineness of notarized documents.

A still further development in the utilization of documentary evidence, which resulted from the institution of notaries, was the permanent proof value accorded to such documents. For if the document was attacked after the notary who signed it had died, then the proponent of the disputed instrument could evince its genuineness, if by comparison with other writings which stood acknowledged as those of the deceased notary a uniform likeness was manifest in the sundry documents. The procedure of the

---

[32] *Capitularia Regum Francorum*, I, 9, 13, in *MGH., Leges*, I, 22.

[33] Brunner, *Deutsche Rechtsgeschichte*, I, 306.

[34] Brunner, *loc. cit.*

[35] *Op. cit.*, I, 489.

[36] *Lex Ribuaria*, 59, 5, in *MGH., Leges*, V, 249. Cf. also Bresslau, *loc. cit.*

comparison was carried out in the following manner: The disputed document was placed on the altar with two other writings made by the designated notary. The chancellor, a public official of the King's court, acting as expert, examined the writings. If the signature in the disputed document agreed with the signatures in the other writings of the notary, the chancellor placed his right hand upon the disputed instrument. By this act the genuineness of the document was established. This was sufficient to give it the value and efficacy of furnishing complete proof.[37] The chronicles of the court procedure testify that this practice was inforced in the Ribuarian, Salic and Alemannic jurisdictions.[38] Thus the permanent value of documents which were executed by notaries, and which were proved to be genuine when they were compared with other writings that were duly acknowledged, came to be recognized rather generally among the Germanic peoples. But documentary evidence as a means of proof always remained a subsidiary agency. For, in the event that the notaries and those who witnessed their writings were still alive, it was demanded of them to acknowledge the documents which had been executed or signed by them. Only upon their death did such instruments acquire a probative value of themselves. This legal fact was one of considerable importance, however, for it guaranteed the permanency of legal transactions beyond the life time of those who could have furnished direct testimony as witnesses in support of the genuine character of the documents.

This privileged character of documents in their full and independent probative value was of short duration. With the division of the Carlovingian monarchy, which foreshadowed the future kingdoms of France and Germany, the inborn distrust of the Germanic peoples for documentary evidence again manifested itself and caused the rapid decline of this institution among them. Later it was revived through Italian influence. From the second half of the tenth century, consequently, no reference is made of public notaries, except, in a few instances, of those who served the King.

---

[37] Bresslau, *op. cit.*, I, 488.

[38] Bresslau, *loc. cit.*

There was a return to the former practice which permitted one to choose whomever he pleased to draw up the document for him.[39]

An exception, however, is found in the practice of the Church. The prescription of Charles the Great in the year 805, which ordered every bishop and abbot to have his own chancellor or notary,[40] was preserved even among the Germanic nations.[41] Occasionally these ecclesiastical notaries drew up documents for the people. But in the year 813 the Council of Chalon-sur-Saône forbade priests to exercise the office of public chancellor or notary.[42]

---

[39] Bresslau, *op. cit.*, I, 446.

[40] *Capitularia Regum Francorum,* I, 49, 10, in *MGH., Leges,* I, 132.

[41] Many examples are given by Bresslau, *op. cit.*, I, 446 sq.

[42] This prohibition is mentioned in canon 44 of this Council. Cf. Mansi, *Sacrorum Conciliorum Nova et Amplissima Collectio* (53 vols. in 59, Paris, Arnhem, Leipzig, 1901-1927), XIV, 102; Hardouin, *Conciliorum Collectio Regia Maxima* (12 vols., Parisiis, 1715), IV, 1039.

CHAPTER IV

Documentary Evidence in the Corpus Iuris Canonici

ARTICLE I. THE USE AND VALUE OF DOCUMENTS

The middle ages witnessed the fusion of the Roman and Germanic legal elements which dealt with the matter of judicial evidence. Heretofore the systems of acquiring evidence and of establishing proof had been as varied as the peoples themselves. This merging was accomplished by legally minded and capable Popes, chief of whom were Alexander III (+ 1181), Innocent III (+ 1216), Honorius III (+ 1227), Gregory IX (+ 1241), Innocent IV (+ 1254), Nicholas III (+ 1280), and Clement V (+ 1314). Through their aid especially a happy medium between the latitude permitted to judges by Roman law and the strict rigidity of the Germanic law has been introduced into Canon Law. By the close contact and influence of the Church, many barbarous customs which were inherently wrong and prevalent in the early middle ages, such as forensic duels and ordeals by fire and water, were slowly but effectually eliminated, and in their stead more rational methods were adopted.[1] Thus the better elements of the Roman and Germanic processual law have been adopted by the Church, and with the addition of new and distinctive methods of her own a more satisfactory and rational method of obtaining proof has developed.

One of the cogent means of proof accepted in Canon Law from Roman Law was the decisory or suppletory oath. These oaths were employed when documentary or testamentary proof was lacking or judged insufficient.[2]

---

[1] C. 2, c. XXXIII, q. 1; c. 5, X, *de frigidis et maleficiatis, et impotentia coeundi,* IV, 15; c. 5, 7, 8, 9, 13, X, *de purgatione canonica,* V, 34.

[2] A *suppletory* oath was one which the judge could tender to one of the parties; a *decisory* oath was one which one of the litigants could tender to the other party with the permission of the judge.

Although the oath was given extensive use and importance in the adjudication of trials, the canonists of this period, bearing in mind the great sanctity and reverence of the oath, inveighed against its excessive and unnecessary use. Pope Alexander III permitted the oath to be employed when other means of proof were lacking, but declared that a plaintiff who had fully proved his case through documents or witnesses should not be compelled to take the oath.[3]

This decree of Pope Alexander III has an important bearing on the topic under discussion. For it shows that documents as well as the testimonies of witnesses were regarded as having the value of full and complete proof in court.

Later Pope Innocent III, while asserting the general principle of equality of proof by documents and by the testimony of witnesses, stated that not every instrument has the same value as the testimony of three or more trustworthy witnesses.[4] This is indicative of the fact that not all writings were accorded the same probative value. But they were evaluated according to their external characteristics, which characteristics led to the presumption of their intrinsic worth. That a document furnish the same proof as the testimony of three or more trustworthy witnesses (*plenam fidem*) it was necessary that it be either a public or an authenticated private document, and in either case the instrument could not be under the suspicion of fraud or deceit.

A public document was one drawn up by a public notary with the due solemnities. Such an instrument, of itself, furnished the value of full proof even beyond the lifetime of the testamentary witnesses.[5] This was but a natural consequence. For such a document gave rise to a twofold presumption in favor of the genuine-

---

[3] C. 2, X, *de probationibus,* II, 19: "Sane quoniam apud vos consuetum esse didicimus, ut, cum aliquis intentionem suam fundaverit instrumentis, aut testibus, ei sacramentum nihilominus deferatur, quod si subire noluerit, fides probationibus non habetur: Nos (cum tunc demum ad huiusmodi sit suffragium recurrendum cum aliae legitimae probationes deesse noscuntur), talem consuetudinem reprobamus." Cf. also c. 2, X, *de fide instrumentorum,* II, 22.

[4] C. 10, X, *de fide instrumentorum,* II, 22.

[5] C. 2, X, *de fide instrumentorum,* II, 22: "Scripta vero authentica, si testes inscripti decesserint, nisi per manum publicam facta fuerint, ita, quod appareant publica . . . non videntur nobis alicuius firmitatis robur habere." Cf. also c. 3, C. 12, q. 2.

ness of the instrument, namely, a) from the quality of the person of the notary who had been chosen and appointed by public authority with the added fact that on assuming his office he took an oath to perform his duty faithfully, and b) from the fact that the required solemnities for a public document aided in removing the suspicion of fraud. Hence, since the purpose of the means of proof was and is to convince the mind of the judge, no supplementary proof was necessary.[6]

This did not, however, relieve the judge of his duty to investigate and pass judgment on the genuineness of the documents, nor did it curtail the right of parties to contest their genuineness and integrity. For documents, as will be seen later,[7] whose integrity and genuineness are doubted can not produce any certainty in the mind of the judge, and consequently remain without probative value.

All documents that were not public were private. Private documents were all those which were not originally drawn up by or in the presence of a public person. There was a distinction made, however, between authentic and non-authentic private documents. An authentic private instrument was indeed private by its very nature, but was accorded a special status in judicial value by a public recognition of its genuineness. In the Decretal law, considered in its final shape, documents could obtain this public recognition or could be authenticated in the following manner: a) through the signature of the one who drew up the document along with the signature of three trustworthy witnesses who were his contemporaries and could appear in court and furnish proof that they inscribed their names to the instrument;[8] b) through the authentic seal of a bishop, civil magistrate, judge, or any one whose office gave him the right to use a public seal;[9] d) through the fact of their being faithfully preserved in public archives;[10] e) through

[6] Reg. 31, R. J., in VI°: "Eum, qui certus est, certiorari ulterius non oportet."

[7] Cf. *infra*, p.

[8] "Scripta vero authentica, si testes inscripti decesserint . . . non videntur nobis alicuius firmitatis robur habere."—C. 2, X, *de fide instrumentorum*, II, 22.

[9] "Nisi . . . authenticum sigillum habuerint."—*Loc. cit.*

[10] C. 1, C. XXX, q. 1.

the fact of their being judicial acts, that is, the minutes and records of judicial proceedings written by persons appointed by the court, even though these were not notaries;[11] f) through the fact that they were drawn up in the manner recognized by custom as giving them an authentic or public character, for custom could render authentic a document which otherwise would be considered merely private.[12]

What has been said concerning the force of public instruments proper applied equally to authentic private instruments until the promulgation of the Code.[13] In other words, they of themselves, without any corroborative evidence, produced full and complete proof in court.[14]

It should be noted here that the original and not merely the copy of the document had to be produced, except when the copy was lawfully or properly taken from the original by a public person.[15]

The Decretals are in perfect harmony with Roman Law regarding the legal efficacy of non-authentic private documents, namely, they do not have any probative value either in favor of the one who drew them up or against a third party.[16] They furnished full proof against the one who drew them up only when he acknowl-

---

[11] C. 11, X, *de probationibus,* II, 19. The Code includes these among the public ecclesiastical documents. Cf. canon 1813, § 1, n. 3. They must, however, be transcribed or at least signed by a qualified notary or actuary. Cf. *infra,* p.

[12] "Respondemus quod si consuetudo illius patriae obtinet approbata, ut instrumentis illius regis fides adhibeatur, vos ea secure poteritis admittere." —C. 9, X, *de fide instrumentorum,* II, 22. Cf. also c. 11, X, *de aetate et qualitate, et ordine praeficiendorum,* I, 14.

[13] Cf. *infra,* p.

[14] C. 2, X, *de fide instrumentorum,* II, 22.

[15] "Si scripturam authenticam non videmus, ad exemplaria nihil facere possumus."—C. 1, X, *de fide instrumentorum,* II, 22. "Si instrumenta propter vetustatem, vel propter aliam iustam causam exemplari petantur, coram ordinario iudice vel delegato ab eo specialiter presententur: qui si ea diligenter inspecta in nulla sui parte vitiata repererit, per publicam personam illa praecipiat exemplari, eandem authoritatem per hoc cum originalibus habitura."—C. 16, X, *de fide instrumentorum,* II, 22. Cf. also c. 4, X, *de confirmatione utili vel inutili,* II, 30.

[16] C. 10, X, *de fide instrumentorum,* II, 22; compare with C. (4, 19) 5, in the *Corpus Iuris Civilis.*

edged them as his own or as signed by himself.[17] In case he denied having written them their genuineness had to be proved by other means, e.g., by comparison of handwriting, or by competent witnesses who testified that they were present and saw him write the disputed document.

The value accorded to public civil documents was not until the Code[18] defined with uniform accuracy. However, Innocent III, in reply to a question concerning a case arising in Scotland, wrote that documents issuing from the Scottish King might be securely relied upon in the diocesan court, provided that the custom of that country held such papers as authentic for ecclesiastical courts.[19]

ARTICLE II. THE USE AND VALUE OF DEFECTIVE DOCUMENTS

It was stated above that parties had the right to contest the genuineness and integrity of documents regardless of their character or nature. Documents could be impugned or called in question on two counts: namely, a) either as spurious documents, or b) as documents containing false statements. Thus a document became suspected of being forged, and consequently its genuineness could be called in question when it was drawn up without the formalities required at the time and in the place of composition,[20] or when it was not properly authenticated.[21] Even when an instrument was conceded to be genuine, it could still be attacked as containing misrepresentations, or even false statements, totally at variance with the real facts of the case. For it can easily be understood that the writer of an instrument, even though he was a public official, could either inadvertently or even maliciously misrepresent the transaction recorded by him. Consequently, when it was shown by some means, as by the oath of a party, by other documents, by expert inspection or by the testimony of witnesses, preferably the documentary witnesses themselves,[22] that the docu-

---

[17] C. 10, X, *de probationibus,* II, 19.
[18] Canon 1814. Cf. *infra,* p.
[19] C. 9, X, *de fide instrumentorum,* II, 22.
[20] Cc. 2, 8, X, *de consuetudine,* I, 4.
[21] C. 6, X, *de fide instrumentorum,* II, 22.
[22] C. 10, X, *de fide instrumentorum,* II, 22.

ment was forged or substantially incorrect, it goes without saying that the probative value of the document could be disclaimed.

In 1203 a question arose whether the elected candidate for the bishopric of Lucca was irregular by reason of an attempted marriage. Among the documents presented to prove the fact of his marriage was one sent by the Archpriest of Lucca which had apparently been signed by the greater part of the Chapter. Innocent rejected the document on the testimony of these men that they knew nothing of such a document.[23]

Moreover, one document could be employed against another. If they were mutually contrary regarding the same matter, they destroyed each other's probative value, unless one was shown to have been forged or unauthentic.[24]

Documents could also be questioned in view of the erasures, interpolations, or corrections contained in them. The decision of the above questions rested with the judge, for he it was who had to determine, to his own satisfaction, the actual truth in the matter. If a document had been subjected to such erasures, interpolations, or corrections, that its meaning or genuineness was left open to serious doubt, the judge was forced to consider it as having no value for the case at issue.[25]

However, Pope Innocent III warned the judge not lightly to discard documents because of erasures or corrections as long as the proper and original sense of the document could not be misunderstood.[26]

Public documents could not generally be contested or sustained by the oath of the parties.[27]

---

[23] C. 33, X, *de testibus et attestationibus,* II, 20.

[24] C. 13, X, *de fide instrumentorum,* II, 22.

[25] C. 6, X, *de fide instrumentorum,* II, 22; c. 7, X, *de religiosis domibus ut episcopo sint subiectae,* III, 36.

[26] C. 9, X, *de crimine falsi,* V, 20: "Verum nos literas ipsas, quae redargutae fuerant falsitatis, diligentius intuentes, nullum in eis falsitatis signum vel suspicionis invenimus, nisi paucarum literarum rasuras, quae nequaquam sapientis animum in dubitationem vertere debuerunt." Cf. also Cc. 5, 6, X, *de testibus et attestationibus,* II, 20; cc. 3, 6, X, *de fide instrumentorum,* II, 22.

[27] C. 2, X, *de probationibus,* II, 19.

CHAPTER V

Documentary Evidence from the Corpus Iuris Canonici to the Code of Canon Law

Documentary evidence, which had in former times played an important part in procedure, but later fell into disuse, began again to obtain a position of real proof-means, and about the year 1200, owing to the increase of commerce, appeared to be superior to the evidence furnished by the testimony of witnesses. At this time the rule was adopted that, once the genuineness of a document was admitted or successfully proved, its content was no longer open to dispute.[1] This was unlike Roman law which permitted the one against whom a document had once been produced and declared genuine by the court to demand the document to be produced again, in order that he might attempt to prove that it had been forged. Before he was permitted to demand its production the second time, he was first required to take an oath to the effect that he thought he could prove it had been forged. In case the one who had first requested the declaration of genuineness by the court asserted that he was unable to produce the document again because he had been deprived of it by accident, he was, in turn, required to swear that he did not have the said document in his possession; that he did not give it to another; that it was not held by another with his consent; and that he had not been guilty of fraud to prevent its appearance, but, that the document had actually been lost without his fault and hence it was impossible to produce it a second time. In the event he took an oath to the above statements, he was excused from the necessity of producing the document. But if he refused to take the oath as demanded, then the former decision of the court was revoked, and the instrument was considered as forged and of no value against him to whose detriment

[1] Millar, "Method of the Proceedings," *The Continental Legal History Series* (10 vols., Boston: Little, Brown, and Company, 1912-1927), VII (1927), 125-178) especially 162. This series is henceforth cited *CLHS*.

it had originally been produced.[2] Moreover, Roman Law,[3] and subsequent to this period Canon Law as well,[4] permitted the defendant to attempt to prove that the document which was produced against him, if it otherwise possessed all the marks of genuineness and authenticity, did not correctly state his intention at the time the said document was executed.

During the latter middle ages the custom of drawing up agreements in writing became more and more widespread to the almost entire exclusion of the instrumentality of witnesses. However, private writings did not acquire any probative force except by virtue of an acknowledgment or confession in court on the part of the one who signed them. The deed under private seal did not prove its own date, as far as third parties were concerned, unless it bore the official stamp.[5]

In the year 1368 the Council of Lavaur decreed that in all contracts granting an emphyteusis or creating a vassal, when ecclesiastical goods were concerned, two public documents should be drawn up, one of which was to be held by the ecclesiastical lord, the other by the vassal or tenant.[6]

During this time, when documents had obtained such an important place in commercial dealings, the office of notary grew in importance. However, from later councils it can be learned that abuses crept in and that some were assuming the title and acting as notaries without the proper authority or qualifications.

A Synod held in the Province of Prague in the year 1355 deplored the fact that many illiterate persons were ignorantly drawing up their own documents, while others, falsely assuming the

---

[2] C. (4, 21) 20.

[3] Nov. 44, Pr.

[4] Pallottini, *Collectio omnium Conclusionum et Resolutionum Congregationis Concilii ab anno 1564 ad annum 1860* (18 vols., Romae, 1868-1895), X, v. "Instrumentum," n. 8.

[5] Brissaud, "Contracts, Feudal Period," *CLHS*, III (1912), 491-512.

[6] Can. 41: "Statuimus insuper et perpetuo ordinamus, quod de omnibus contractibus, tam vassallaticis quam emphiteotecariis, rerum ecclesiasticarum, infra nostras provincias deinceps duo fiant necessario publica instrumenta per alphabetum divisa: quorum unum penes se habeat dominus ecclesiasticus, et alteram vassalus seu emphiteota."—Mansi, *Sacrorum Conciliorum et amplissima collectio,* XXVI, 506.

title of public notaries, presumed to execute instruments from which many inconveniences and dangers resulted. With the view to correcting these abuses the Synod decreed that no one should be permitted to act as a public notary or to execute any kind of instrument whatsoever before he proved that he had been instituted in his office by the bishop or his delegate. The Synod further decreed that if anyone acted contrary to this provision he should be excommunicated and the document drawn up by him was to be considered as having no value.[7]

This decree was repeated by the Council of Magdeburg held in 1370[8] and again in 1403 by another Council of Magdeburg.[9]

The Synod of Passau held in the year 1470 enacted a similar decree by stating that no one offering to act as a public notary should, under any circumstances, be admitted and no credence should be given to a document drawn up by him, unless he first presented himself before the bishop or his delegate and proved that he had been legitimately constituted in his office.[10]

Despite all these provisions, it seems that the abuse was not corrected. For in the year 1491 the Council of Bamberg stated that there were some in Holy Orders exercising the office of notary, and that their documents were considered as giving full proof not only in civil dealings but also in ecclesiastical affairs, although their authority and other qualifications to act as such were questionable. Whereupon this Council decreed that any one exercising the office of public notary, either in the city or in the diocese, should not be admitted and his documents should not be accepted as public unless he showed by whose authority he held

---

[7] Can. 24: ". . . Contrarium faciens, excommunicationis sententiam incidat, et instrumenta per eum confecta, sint irrita ipso facto."—Hartzheim, *Concilia Germaniae* (11 vols., Coloniae Augustae Agrippinsensium, 1759-1790), IV, 387.

[8] *Ibidem,* IV, 420.

[9] *Ibidem,* V, 685.

[10] Tit. XIII: "Placuit nostrae Sanctae Synodo, ut nullus se publicum Notarium afferens in officio tabellionatus aliqualiter admittatur, nec credatur ejus instrumentum, nisi coram Nobis, aut nostris Officialibus, vel eorum vicegerentibus de suo officio plenam faciet fidem. Quoniam saepe ex Notariis incognitis, et imperitis gravia solent pericula evenire."—*Ibidem,* V, 479.

the office of notary, and that he had the other necessary qualifications.[11]

These qualifications were more specifically determined by a Synod of Hildesheim in 1539. In this Synod it was decreed that, in order to conform to the statutes recently made in Cologne, one who did not have sufficient education, did not enjoy a good reputation, and had not completed his twenty-third year of age, should not be permitted to hold the office of notary. The judgment as to whether or not a person had these necessary qualifications was left to the bishops themselves. This Synod further provided that documents drawn up by those acting contrary to this ruling had to be rejected, since they were invalid and had no force or importance and could not be admitted in or outside of court in any way whatsoever.[12]

The decrees of the Councils here cited can not fail to show the exaggerated importance that was attached both to ecclesiastical and to civil documents. They show further that the exaggerated importance attributed to written evidence during this period gave rise to the many abuses against which the Fathers of the Councils legislated with seemingly little effect. Consequently, about the middle of the fifteenth century, owing to the influence of the School of Bologna, there was a tendency to return to the practice of proof through the testimony of witnesses, although many of the civil Codes contained statutes, either proscribing witnesses or causing them to be held in great suspicion,[13] while authentic documents, in many Codes, constituted a certain full and absolute proof.[14]

Lega states that, for a while, after the influence of this School was felt, witnesses were restored to their former place in the civil procedure, but that in view of corruption, such as bribery and threats which were held out to witnesses, it was difficult to obtain the truth, and that consequently the use of witnesses was greatly distrusted. For this reason limitations were again put on witnesses, and in the year 1566 in France, under the reign of Charles IX, the ordinance of Moulins, Art. 54, decreed that a contract had to be

[11] Tit. XIV—*Ibidem,* V, 603.

[12] Cap. XII—*Ibidem,* VI, 319.

[13] Lega, *De Iudiciis Ecclesiasticis Civilibus,* I, n. 473.

[14] Roberti, *De Processibus,* II, n. 334.

drawn up for every financial consideration which exceeded one hundred pounds in value.[15] The Ordinance read: "Concerning everything exceeding the value of 100 pounds contracts shall be drawn up before notaries . . . without receiving any proof by witnesses excepting as to the contents of the contract, and without receiving any proof as to that which may be alleged to have been said or agreed upon before the contract, then and afterwards."[16] This is similar to the Statute of Frauds enacted in England on April 16, 1677, which later became an interwoven part of American law and is in force generally throughout the American jurisdictions at the present time.[17] The Ordinance of Louis XIV in the year 1667 retained a like disposition, as did also the Napoleonic Code as well as all the Codes derived from it.[18]

That the Church's practice concerning the use and evaluation of documents was at the time very similar to that of the civil law, is evidenced by declarations of the Sacred Congregation of the Council.

On March 26, 1783, the Sacred Congregation expressly stated that, in the line of proof, public documents were to be preferred to witnesses.[19] Again on September 20, 1794, in a case of a disputed legacy, which had been left to one party by means of a document and was alleged to have been given to another by way of promise expressed merely in words, the Congregation decided in favor of the possessor of the document, stating that the authority of a public instrument was far greater than that of an assertion.[20] Still in another case wherein presumption was alleged against a public instrument the Congregation on August 2, 1823, declared

---

[15] Lega, *op. cit.*, n. 473.

[16] This Ordinance is translated and quoted by Brissaud in the *CLHS*, III, 511, note 6.

[17] Bays, *Cases and Materials on Business Law* (4. ed., Chicago: Callaghan and Company, 1939), p. 279 sq.

[18] Roberti, *loc. cit.*

[19] "Instrumenta publica in linea probationis praeferuntur Testibus."—Pallottini, *Collectio omnium Conclusionum et Resolutionum Congregationis Concilii*, X, v. "Instrumentum," n. 1.

[20] "Hinc multo magis assertioni auctoritas praevalet publici instrumenti."—*Ibidem*, n. 3.

that only the most absolute and evident proofs may be offered against a public document.[21]

This last decision of the Sacred Congregation is especially important to note, for it admits at least some proofs against a public document. In fact, a few years previously (1788) the Sacred Congregation—while mentioning the fact that in the civil law of Spain a public document, if it was drawn up by a notary of good reputation who acknowledged the document as his own, remained valid even if the documentary witnesses stated the contrary—expressly stated that in Canon Law the testimony of the witnesses prevailed if they contradicted the written instrument in which the signature of their names appeared.[22] This was a return to the principle of the Decretal Law.[23]

Though not contained in the Church's legislation, nor ever having the force of law in Canon Law courts, the *Regolamento legislative e giudiciario,* promulgated in 1834 by Gregory XVI for the use of all secular tribunals of the Papal States,[24] did exert great influence as a norm for canonical procedure.[25]

This law of Pope Gregory XVI excluded proofs through the testimony of witnesses if the civil law required written proof, and also if the case had reference to some public act.[26] It furthermore admitted only direct proofs against a public document; in other words, only the genuineness of a document could be denied when the document was brought in court. The same law attributed full proof against the alleged author or signatory of a signed private document until the signature was denied.[27] In case this private written instrument had been acknowledged by the author or signatory before a notary or in court its value as proof was

---

[21] ". . . adversus publicum instrumentum luculentissimae, et numeris omnibus absolutissimae probationes sunt afferendae."—*Ibidem,* n. 4.

[22] "De iure autem Canonico—si testes contradicunt instrumento, in quo scripti sunt, praevalent instrumento."—*Ibidem,* n. 6.

[23] C. 33, X, *de probationibus,* II, 19.

[24] *Regolamento legislative e giudiciario,* found in the *Acta Gregorii Papae XVI* (4 vols., Romae, 1901-1904), IV, 300-410.

[25] Lega, *De Iudiciis Ecclesiasticis Civilibus,* I, *prooemium,* p. 17, note 2.

[26] *Regolamento,* nn. 830, 839.

[27] *Ibidem,* n. 615.

equivalent to that of a public written instrument.[28] When one was called upon in court to acknowledge or deny the authorship of a document alleged to be his, then, if he did neither of these expressly, the tribunal was instructed to declare such a document as acknowledged.[29] But when he expressly denied its authorship, then the producer of the disputed instrument had to prove its genuineness either by the testimony of reliable witnesses or through a like declaration of experts who were particularly skilled in the art of comparing the disputed handwritings.[30]

---

[28] *Ibidem*, nn. 616, 617.
[29] *Ibidem*, n. 620.
[30] *Ibidem*, n. 802 sq.

PART TWO

Canonical Commentary

CHAPTER VI

NATURE AND KINDS OF DOCUMENTS

ART. I. PUBLIC ECCLESIASTICAL DOCUMENTS

CANON 1813, § 1. Praecipua documenta publica ecclesiastica haec sunt: 1°. Acta Summi Pontificis et Curiae Romanae et Ordinariorum in exercitio suorum munerum authentica forma exarata, itemque attestationes authenticae de iisdem actibus datae ab illis vel eorum notariis.

Different species of instruments drawn up by public authority in the Church are derived from the different nature of the acts and also from the quality and dignity of the persons from whom these instruments emanate. First in order must, therefore, be considered the acts drawn up by the Prelates of the Church for the government of the faithful.

A. Acts of the Supreme Pontiff

Preeminent among the acts emanating from the governing authority of the Church are those of the Supreme Pontiff. They are issued for the government of the Universal Church in the nature of Apostolic Constitutions, of *Motu Proprios,* of Decrees, of Encyclicals and of Apostolic Letters and Epistles, sent out in the form of Bulls, Briefs and Letters.

The present canon states that such acts in order to constitute public documents must be drawn up in an authentic form.[1]

---

[1] "Verba *authentica forma exarata* tum ad acta Ordinariorum, comprehensis utique Ordinariis religiosis, referuntur, tum ad acta Romani Pontificis et Curiae Romanae."—Coronata, *Institutiones,* n. 1342. Cf. also Augustine, *Eccles. Trials,* p. 255; Eichmann, *Das Prozesszrecht des C. I. C.,* p. 155.

There is no common rule regulating the requirements for the authentic form of documents, for in practice each species of written instruments has its proper mode of authentication.[2]

Thus it is the general custom that Bulls drawn up in consistory are authenticated by the signature of the Holy Father. The non-consistorial Bulls receive their authentic form either 1) through the signature of the Cardinal Chancellor with that of other officials of the Chancellery, or 2) through the signature of the Cardinal Chancellor and that of the Cardinal Moderator of the competent Congregation, or 3) through that of the Cardinal Secretary of State and that of the Cardinal Moderator of the Congregation, or that of the Cardinal Chancellor, or that of the Cardinal Datary.[3] The Briefs are signed by the Cardinal Secretary of State, or, if they contain matters of less importance, by the Chancellor of Briefs.[4] The Letters sent out by the Secretariate of Briefs and by the Secretariate of Latin Letters bear the signature of the Supreme Pontiff. The mention of the date, the indication of the place of issuance and the affixing of the proper seal are all incorporated in the aforesaid documents.[5] The above acts, in so far as they are of public law, are officially promulgated and have the

---

[2] "Quaenam sit authentica forma non potest explicari communi regula. Sane quod pertinet ad solemnitatem, nulla habetur ex iure *communi; iure peculiari* Curiae Romanae, servandae sunt constitutiones ordinantes formam actorum ab eadem promanantium: can. 242-264. Pro Curiis dioecesanis servandi sunt can. 363-365 ubi personarum in eisdem certa munera et diversae attributiones habentur, determinatur potestas et officium. Una tantum est certa regula nempe qui potestate utitur ordinaria regiminis de suis actis scripto exaratis et sua subscriptione munitis fidem publicam facere eisdem publicam auctoritatem tribuere. Qui potestate ordinaria aut legitime delegata non pollet recurrat oportet ad operam notarii: can. 373, § 1; ubi dictio *'quorum scriptura* vel *subscriptio fidem facit'* intelligitur comprehendere, scripturam ab eis ex integro exaratam et *subscriptam* aut *simplicem subscriptionem,* fidem facere publicam."—Lega-Bartoccetti, *Commentarius,* II, p. 784, note 1.

[3] Roberti, *De Processibus,* II, n. 367, p. 95.

[4] *Ibidem,* p. 96.

[5] *Loc. cit.;* cf. also Maroto, *Institutiones iuris canonici,* n. 338; Wernz-Vidal, *Ius Canonicum,* VI, n. 509; Muniz, *Procedimientos Eclesiásticos,* III, n. 362.

force of law by their insertion in the *Acta Apostolicae Sedis,* which constitutes the official *Commentarium* of the Holy See.[6]

The authentic means of proving the genuineness of a Pontifical *Oraculum vivae vocis* is the testimony of a Cardinal of the Roman Curia.[7] An attestation written and signed by a Cardinal is a public document proving the concession of a privilege, fact or resolution given in that *Oraculum.*

Likewise, the authentic attestations concerning the above acts given by the persons from whom the original act emanated, or by their notaries[8] or other officials appointed for this purpose,[9] are by virtue of the present canon considered public ecclesiastical documents.[10]

By virtue of canon 1683[11] acts or instruments which have received the confirmation of the Roman Pontiff in the so-called *forma specifica*[12] are to be included among the acts of the Supreme Pontiff. For such a confirmation raises the act or document thus confirmed to the state of a papal act or document by appropriation, and all defects of the original act or instrument are thereby healed.[13] A further effect resulting from this confirmation, as canon 1863 indicates, is that such an act or instrument cannot be

---

[6] Canon 9.

[7] Canon 239, § 1, 17o.

[8] By apostolic notaries, when there is question of the documents of the Roman Pontiff or of the Roman Curia; by the notaries of the ordinary, when there is question of acts executed by authorities inferior to that of the Holy See.

[9] E.g., officials of the Apostolic Chancery, Datary and Camera.

[10] Wernz-Vidal, *Ius Canonicum,* VI, n. 509, p. 452.

[11] "Iudex inferior de confirmatione, a Romano Pontifice actui vel instrumento-adiecta, videre non potest, nisi Apostolicae Sedis praecesserit mandatum."

[12] "Hic agitur de confirmatione in forma specifica, a solo Romano Pontifice concessa, exclusis ceteris dicasteriis romanis nisi ad hoc habeant mandatum speciale."—Beste, *Introductio in Codicem,* p. 787; Coronata, *Institutiones,* n. 1211. "Confirmatio in forma specifica, quae fit cum perfecta notitia singulorum actorum et decretorum, vel, uti dicitur, motu proprio et ex certa scientia, et efficit, ut decreta conciliaria transformentur et inducant naturam legis pontificiae ideoque, si forte ultra concilii vires lata fuerint, obtinent valorem et firmitatem."—Beste, *op. cit.,* p. 255.

[13] Cf. Woywod, *A Practical Commentary on the Code of Canon Law* (2 vols., New York: Joseph F. Wagner, 1932), II, 240.

judged by a lower court, including the Sacred Congregations and Tribunals of the Roman Curia,[14] except with the special mandate of the Supreme Pontiff himself. This latter clause safeguards both the authority of the supreme judge and the administration of justice.

B. Acts of the Roman Curia

Next in importance and dignity are the acts emanating from the Roman Curia. All these acts are published in the name of the respective Sacred Congregation, Tribunal, Office or Pontifical Commission, but the more important of these acts must first have the approval of the Roman Pontiff.[15]

The documents of the Sacred Congregations are published under the form of decrees, rescripts, letters and solutions of doubts. The decrees are authenticated by the signature of the Cardinal Moderator—or of another Cardinal in the absence of a Moderator—[16] and the Secretary[17] of the Congregation or of his substitute. Ordinarily the rescripts are signed by the same officials who sign the decrees, but they may be signed by a Sub-secretary. The letters are signed by the Cardinal Moderator and the Secretary, or at least by one of the two. The signature of the Secretary along with the imprint of the seal of the Sacred Congrega-

---

[14] Coronata, *Institutiones,* n. 1211, p. 117.

[15] "Nothing of importance or of an extraordinary character is to be decided by the Sacred Congregations, Tribunals and Offices without the president of the respective committee having notified the Roman Pontiff. All concessions and resolutions need the Papal approval, except those affairs for which special faculties have been given to the presidents of the Offices, Tribunals and Congregations, and excepting the sentences of the Tribunals of the Roman Rota and Apostolic Signatura."—Canon 244 as translated by Woywod, *A Practical Commentary on the Code of Canon Law,* I, 95. Cf. also Wernz-Vidal, *Ius Canonicum,* VI, n. 509, II; Muniz, *Procedimientos Eclesiásticos,* III, n. 363.

[16] The Moderator's official title is that of Cardinal Prefect of the Congregation, unless the Roman Pontiff himself is Prefect of the Congregation. In the latter case one of the older Cardinals of the Sacred College is designated by the Pope to discharge the office of Secretary and the Cardinal thus designated signs the documents under that title.

[17] Assessor in the event the Roman Pontiff is Prefect of the Congregation.

tion gives the authentic form to the solutions of doubts. It is to be noted, however, that documents of the Holy Office are often signed by the notary alone. Likewise, dispensations of minor importance granted by the Sacred Congregation of the Sacraments are signed solely by the Secretary or even by a lesser official.[18]

The documents of the Pontifical Commissions are signed by the Cardinal Prefect and the Secretary, or at times simply by the Secretary.

Regarding the acts of the Tribunals, the acts of the *Signatura Apostolica* are signed by the Secretary and Notary, excepting the sentences which have the signatures of the *Praelatus Votans,* of the Secretary, who signs under the word *Visa,* and of the Notary. The Dean of the Sacred Roman Rota signs its official enactments. The *Iudex Ponens* and the Notary sign the edictal citations; the sentences, sent out for execution, are signed by the *Iudex Ponens,* the associate judges and the Notary. In the Sacred Penitentiary the acts are signed by either the Cardinal Major Penitentiary or the Regent.

The documents of the Apostolic Chancery, Datary and Camera are signed by the respective presiding Cardinals and by the Secretary or the Regent. All the documents emanating from the organs of the Roman Curia are sealed and dated.[19]

The acts of the Roman Curia which are of public law, like those of the Supreme Pontiff, are officially promulgated with their insertion in the *Acta Apostolicae Sedis.*[20]

C. *Acts of Lesser Ordinaries*

Under this heading are included the documents of lesser ordinaries[21] according to their degree of participation in the legislative, administrative and judicial powers, if and when they act in the exercise of their office and in as far as the documents are drawn up in authentic form.

---

[18] Roberti, *De Processibus,* II, n. 367, p. 96. Cf. also Wernz-Vidal, *Ius Canonicum,* VI, n. 509, II.

[19] Roberti, *De Processibus,* II, n. 367, p. 96; Wernz-Vidal, *Ius Canonicum,* VI, n. 509, II; Muniz, *Procedimientos Eclesiásticos,* III, n. 363; Maroto, *Institutiones Iuris Canonici,* n. 338.

[20] Canon 9.

[21] As they are listed in canon 198, § 1.

As has been noted above,[22] it can be learned whether or not a person is acting in his official capacity: 1) from the nature of the business concerning which the document treats, inasfar as the execution thereof pertains to the person by reason of the rights and obligations of his office; 2) from the addition of the signature of any official of the curia; 3) from the expressed declaration by that person affixed to the document; 4) from the use of the seal of the office. The use of the official seal is the most common means of determining that the writer was acting in his official capacity.

Outside of the Roman Curia it seems that each curia may follow its own practice in the matter of establishing the requirements for the validity or for the authentic form of its public documents. For, in fact, as Wernz-Vidal remark, there is no identical form which is observed in all the diocesan curiae for the drawing up of original written instruments.[23] In practice there is a distinction made between the more solemn and the less solemn acts. The more solemn acts are authenticated by the signature of the ordinary and of the chancellor, or of another notary together with the affixing of the proper seal. The less solemn acts seem to have a sufficient mark of authentication in the signature of the ordinary or of a notary together with the affixed seal.[24] Coronata, however, states that the minimum requirement for drawing up any public document in authentic form seems to be at least the signature of the author or of the notary.[25]

The inventories which the bishops are obliged to make by virtue of canon 1299, § 3 and 1483, § 3, must be classed among the public ecclesiastical documents, provided, of course, that it is certain from the signature of the bishop, or that of the chancellor or notary, that these inventories have been made and are acknowledged by the authority of the bishop.[26]

---

[22] P.

[23] *Ius Canonicum,* VI, n. 509, III; Muniz (*Procedimientos Eclesiásticos,* III, n. 364) suggests that fixed norms should be established in provincial councils.

[24] Wernz-Vidal, *Ius Canonicum,* VI, n. 509, III.

[25] *Institutiones,* n. 1342.

[26] Lega-Bartoccetti, *Commentarius,* II, 785.

D. Acts of Ecclesiastical Notaries

CANON 1813, § 1 . . .
2°. Instrumenta a notariis ecclesiasticis confecta.[27]

It should be noted that the original acts of notaries are to be understood here, and not the attestations or copies that may be made by them. For in the latter case the attestations of notaries do not change the juridical nature of the original written instrument.[28]

In the term "notary" is also included the actuary[29] and the chancellor.[30] It is evident from canon 374, § 2 that a notary, in order to act validly, must be legitimately appointed and that the acts drawn up by him are within the scope of his appointment both as to matter and place. Furthermore, he must not be deprived of his capacity to perform legitimate ecclesiastical acts.[31]

It may not be out of place here to recall the fact that religious ordinaries can also according to the present law appoint notaries for the ecclesiastical affairs of their respective religious organizations.[32] However, they may not validly exercise the office of notary or actuary in the processes of beatification and canonization, except in the case of necessity, and even then in the cases which pertain to their own community they are always to be excluded.[33]

That the acts which are set down in writing or which are composed by notaries must be classed among public documents is a natural consequence of the nature of the office and power enjoyed

---

[27] "Iisdem aequiparantur mandata subscripta a parochis ad constituendum procuratorem ad lites (c. 1659, § 2) vel ad celebrandum matrimonium (c. 1089, § 1), etc."—Roberti, *De Processibus,* II, n. 367, p. 97.

[28] *Ibidem,* n. 371, p. 101, note 1.

[29] Canon 1585. The actuary (*actuarius*) gets his name from his office of writing the acts of a trial.

[30] Canon 372, § 3.

[31] Canons 2263 and 2294, § 1. Cf. also Lega, *De Iudiciis Ecclesiasticis Civilibus,* I, n. 154.

[32] Canon 503.

[33] Canon 2014 "Religiosi fungi valide nequeunt munere notarii, nisi ex necessitate; in causis autem propriae religionis semper excluduntur."

by notaries. For a notary is a public authoritative or qualified witness concerning the acts which are done in his presence if he commits them to writing or at least signs these acts when they have been recorded by another.[84]

Such an instrument should bear the seal and the signature of the notary together with the notation of the date and place of issuance, in order that it may be considered a public document.[85]

E. Judicial Ecclesiastical Acts

CANON 1813, § 1 . . .
3°. Acta iudicialia ecclesiastica.

By judicial ecclesiastical acts are understood the records drawn up during the process of an ecclesiastical trial. All these acts—whether they are the *acta causae* (those which relate to the merit of the case, e.g., decisions and all proofs) or the *acta processus* (those which relate to the form of procedure, e.g., summons, declarations or notices, etc.)—must be committed to writing.[86]

The Code is very specific in detailing the authentic form for these acts. For the law states that every page (*folio*) of the acts must be numbered and the signature of the actuary with the seal of the court must appear on each individual page. Furthermore, when an individual act is either completed, or interrupted and thereupon postponed for another session, it is necessary that it be signed by the actuary and the judge (or the presiding judge, if several judges sit in the same case). Whenever the signature of the parties or of the witnesses is required in the judicial acts, and one of the parties or witnesses is unable or refuses to sign his name, a note to that effect must be made in such acts, and the actuary and the judge must attest that the act itself was read

---

[84] Canons 373, § 1; 1791, § 1.

[85] Augustine, *Ecclesiastical Trials*, p. 256. Coronata (*Institutiones*, n. 1342) does not mention the necessity of noting on the document the place of issuance. In his opinion even the noting of the date does not appear essential.—*Ibidem*, n. 1342, p. 247, note 4.

[86] Canon 1585.

verbatim to the party or to the witness, and that the party or witness could not subscribe to the act or refused to do so.[37]

The absolute necessity of a notary is unquestionably evident from canon 1585, in which it is stated that at every trial there must be present a notary who acts as actuary, and that the acts are invalid unless they are drawn up by the notary or are at least signed by him.[38] Consequently, even the acts of the bishop which are drawn up in connection with trials have no force or authority, *si actuarii manu non fuerint exarata vel saltem subscripta.*[39] This latter clause permits the use of a typewriter, but a rubber stamp is not admissible for the signature.[40] Although the law permits two witnesses to supply the presence of a notary in the writing of certain acts,[41] it is the opinion of Coronata that two witnesses can not fulfill the office of the notary in the process of the trial.[42] It should be noted, however, that the acts which the couriers and apparitors write in the execution of their office are public documents.[43]

F. Registers

CANON 1813, § 1 . . .

4°. Inscriptiones baptismi, confirmationis, ordinationis, professionis religiosae, matrimonii, mortis, quae habentur in regestis Curiae vel paroeciae, vel religionis, et attestationes scriptae ex iisdem desumptae et a parochis, vel Ordinariis, vel notariis ecclesiasticis confectae aut earum exemplaria authentica.

---

[37] Canon 1643.

[38] Cf. also canons 1715, § 2; 1778-1780; 1874, § 5; 1882; 2013, § 1.

[39] Lega-Bartoccetti, *Commentarius,* II, 785.

[40] Augustine, *Ecclesiastical Trials,* p. 40.

[41] Cf. e.g., canons 1017, § 1; 1659, § 2; 2143, § 1; 2225; 2309, § 2.

[42] "Vi huius canonis abrogatum censemus ius decretalium quo officium notarii suppleri poterat per duos testes."—*Institutiones,* n. 1123, p. 35. Roberti (*De Processibus,* I, n. 115, p. 187, note 3) is of the same opinion: "Hodie duo testes, quamvis plenam fidem faciant, nequeunt notarium in processu substituere." Wernz-Vidal (*Ius Canonicum,* VI, n. 103, note 49), however, seem to admit the contrary opinion: ". . . evidenter duo isti viri substituendi sunt, si actuarius sive persona publica haberi non possit, . . ."

[43] Canon 1593.

Prior to the enactments of the Council of Trent (1545-1563) concerning parochial registers there were indeed some particular laws concerning this matter and, in general, at least some indefinite measures were taken to secure the maintenance of the parochial books.[44] The Decretalist Nicholaus de Tudeschis (1386-1453), also known as Panormitanus, wrote that such records were considered chiefly as private writings and, as such, did not furnish complete proof.[45] The same Panormitanus, however, made an exception with regard to baptismal registers, since they were reserved in public and faithful custody, and generally were *in nullius praejudicio*.[46]

The Council of Trent in making further and more stringent regulations concerning parochial books at the same time gave them a character similar to that of a public document.[47] On July 3, 1909, the Sacred Congregation of the Council declared that not only the parochial books furnished full proof (*fidem publicam faciunt*), but that likewise the testimonials and copies taken from such registers and signed by either the pastor who administered the sacrament or by his successor have the same probative value. For, so the Congregation of the Council further stated, in such cases the pastor is to be considered a public ecclesiastical notary,

---

[44] O'Rourke, *Parish Registers*, The Catholic University of America Canon Law Studies, n. 88 (Washington, D. C.: The Catholic University of America, 1934), p. 20.

[45] Panormitanus (Nicholaus de Tudeschis), *Commentaria in Quinque Libros Decretalium* (8 vols., in 7, Venetiis, 1578), ad c. 13, X, *de probationibus*, II, 18; Esmein, *Le Mariage en Droit Canonique* (2 vols., 2. ed., Paris: Recueil Sirey, 1929-1935), I, 217-219.

[46] *Loc. cit.*: "Dic ergo quod aut agitur de nullo praejudicio, et tunc scripturae librorum non authenticorum vel scripturae lapidum faciunt fidem, quia tunc sufficiunt probationes non plenae . . . pone exemplum si dubitatur an ecclesia fuerit consecrata, vel infans baptizatus vel simile. Idem puto si factum est antiquissimum et agitur de modico praejudicio . . . Quandoque agitur de magno praejudicio, et tunc aut talis est liber vel scriptura cui ab antiquis nostris communiter creditum est, vel reperitur in loco ubi solum preservantur scripturae antiquae et tales faciunt plenam fidem . . . aut est talis liber vel scriptura cui communiter a majoribus nostris creditum non est nec reperitur in loco ubi solum servantur scripturae authenticae et talis liber vel scriptura facit adminiculum seu praesumptionem, non autem plenam probationem."

[47] Sessio XXIV, de ref. matrim., cc. 1, 2.

who has the right to transcribe authentic copies from the original instrument. But in case these copies were sent to another diocese and especially to distant countries, then with a view to preventing forgery the Sacred Congregation demanded that the signature of the pastor be certified by the ordinary of the pastor who signed such certificates. And if this procedure was not followed the copies were to be considered as having no value.[48]

The Code now directly asserts that the inscriptions of baptism, of confirmation, of ordination, of religious profession, of matrimony and of death, as contained in the registers of the curia, of the parish or of the religious community, as also the written attestations taken from them when made by the pastor, by the ordinary or by ecclesiastical notaries, as well as authentic copies, are to be numbered among the public ecclesiastical records.

It was stated above[49] that a public document is a writing which relates an act that was executed by, or in the presence of, a public official acting as such, and then was committed to writing by the same official. This requisite can not be urged strictly in the case of public registers. For it frequently happens that entries are made in these public registers by persons who indeed witnessed or performed the act, but who are not public persons as defined by the law, or that they are made by public persons who neither witnessed nor performed the act. However, since these registers are in the custody of public persons whose strict duty it is to take care that no entries are made therein which are not true both as to fact and contents, such entries merit the character of public documents.

The present canon clearly distinguishes between attestations and copies. Attestations, as stated before,[50] are writings which relate the sense (*ad sensum*) of the original, while copies are exact (*ad litteram*) transcripts of the original documents. The canon likewise, in some manner, determines who are capable of authenticating these attestations by mentioning ordinaries, pastors[51]

---

[48] S.C.C., *Platien.*, 3 iul. 1909—*AAS*, I (1909), 657-660.

[49] Cf. p.

[50] Cf. p.

[51] A religious superior of a clerical exempt religious in his house performs the duty of pastor. Therefore it seems that he has the same right as a pastor in this matter. Cf. Coronata, *Institutiones*, n. 1342, p. 248.

and ecclesiastical notaries. Thus it seems evident that a civil notary may not authenticate attestations. Regarding copies the Code does not distinguish. As to the question whether assistants or curates are capable of issuing authentic attestations and copies, Coronata, though he is mindful of the stricter opinion of Augustine,[52] nevertheless accords them this right whenever a diocesan statute or a local custom has not expressly restricted their power.[53]

G. Other Public Ecclesiastical Documents

The initial word of canon 1813, *Praecipua,* clearly reveals that the legislator did not intend to enumerate a complete list of public ecclesiastical documents. For besides those listed in the canon there are others that must be considered as such, e.g., those of moral or collegiate persons, recognized at least by the ordinary and acting in a body (*collegialiter*), drawn up in accordance with the proper requirements. Such requirements are the affixing of the official seal and the inscription of the signature of the Superior or Moderator, and, in the absence of a duly elected notary, the additional signature of two witnesses.[54]

ART. II. PUBLIC CIVIL DOCUMENTS

CANON 1813, § 2. Documenta publica civilia ea sunt quae secundum uniuscuiusque loci leges talia iure censentur.

It frequently happens that the Church in her forum must make use of civil documents. As there is a different practice in the

---

[52] *Ecclesiastical Trials,* p. 257.

[53] *Institutiones,* n. 1342, p. 248.

[54] Cf. Coronata, *Institutiones,* n. 1342, note 1; Noval, *De Iudiciis,* n. 545; Wernz-Vidal, *Ius Canonicum,* VI, n. 509, p. 454; Muniz, *Procedimientos Eclesiásticos,* III, n. 368. A stricter opinion is held by Roberti, *De Processibus,* II, n. 367, p. 97:—"Quamvis enumeratio Codicis non sit taxativa (cfr. c. 1813, § 1) haud facile reperiuntur alia acta quibus sit agnoscendus valor documenti publici. Quare non censemus his adnumerandas relationes sacrarum visitationum, acta capitularia, aliaque acta similia, nisi quatenus scripta aut subscripta sint a notario."

various nations and states both as to the nature and value of such documents, the present canon enunciates the general principle that the civil documents are to be judged by the laws of the place in which they are drawn up or used. This principle applies with regard not only to their nature but also to their probative force. For canon 1529 states that whatever the civil law of a country decrees on contracts and payments of all kinds is to be observed also by canon law in ecclesiastical matters, with the same effect, except in so far as the civil law is contrary to the divine law, or as canon law has ruled otherwise. Thus the Code simplifies matters by adopting the civil law in these questions, but at the same time assures the Church's independent right in the questions that pertain to the administration of its ecclesiastical goods.

It is not the writer's purpose to give an extensive treatise on civil documents, for a cursory inspection of the many volumes written on the subject will readily convince the reader that such a task is not within the scope of this work. However, it may prove useful to state some of the general principles of the civil law regarding public documents.

Especially worthy of note is the fact that the quantitative rule of canon law, namely, that a public document or two qualified witnesses beget full proof, is not known in United States civil law procedure. In other words no class of evidence, admissible in law,[55] is conclusive or preferred to other classes that are likewise admissible.

In American civil law, public documents are those made by, or under the direction of, public functionaries in the executive, legislative and judicial departments of the government. Included under this general head are the transactions which officials are required to enter in the books or registers in the course of their public duties, and which, in addition, occur within the scope of their personal knowledge and observation.[56] Wherefore a statement

---

[55] Evidence is admissible when the jury may consider it as part of the evidential material which is to persuade them to the conclusion represented in their verdict. Wigmore, *A Pocket Code of the Rules of Evidence in Trials at Law* (Boston: Little, Brown, and Company, 1910), 14. Hereafter cited by name of author.

[56] *The American and English Encyclopaedia of Law* (30 vols., 2. ed., 1896-1905, New York: Edward Tompson Company), IX (1896), 880.

in writing, made by a public officer, acting under a duty or authority to make the statement, and qualified by personal observation, is admissible. The duty or authority need not be expressly declared but may be implied from the nature of the office. Nor is it necessary that the officer be a person whose sole or main occupation is official, or who has general official duties additional to that of making the statement; but he must be a person having a duty to make the statement by virtue of his occupation and not merely as a mode of providing evidence against himself. Thus a record of marriage, made by a clergyman having a governmental duty to make it, is admissible, even though the clergyman has otherwise no official status. But a record of sales of liquor, made by reason of a statutory duty, is not admissible, because the main object of the statute is to provide a check upon the violation of the law as to liquors. The officer making the statement may be one or more subordinate officers on the staff of the officer who signs it, provided the officer signing the statement or the subordinate acting for him is qualified by personal observation of his own senses,[57] and provided further that, a subordinate using the name or seal of the chief officer is authorized for the purpose.[58]

The various kinds of official documents are classified, with reference to the foregoing principles, into three groups, namely, 1) Registers and Records; 2) Returns and Reports; 3) Certificates.[59]

A register or record is a series of entries on related subjects, made in a single continuous volume or series of volumes, and kept in official custody. Wherever there is a duty for an officer to do or observe a thing, there is implied in law a duty to make a record of what is done or observed, and such a record is admissible. Thus an assessor's record of property assessed is admissible to show the ownership, occupancy, location, and value of the

---

[57] Exceptions to this rule are: 1) a public officer's testimony to the records or acts of his subordinates or predecessors; 2) the use by one person of standard scientific instruments and formulas prepared by another person; 3) the use by an expert of the reported data of fellow-scientists; 4) the report of a medical expert who has taken into consideration the statements of the patient or his attendants; 5) the testimony of one person to the contents of a document read to him by another person.

[58] Wigmore, 252.

[59] *Ibidem*, 253.

property. Likewise a record of marriage, birth, or death, kept by an officer having the duty, or by any other person expressly by law so authorized, is admissible to evidence the matters required to be recorded.[60] A judicial record is a judgment ending a controversy and requiring enforcement without re-inquiry in another court, according to the law of the judgments.[61]

A return or report is a single separate document, made as occasion arises, and kept in official custody,[62] and is admissible if drawn up under the following conditions: 1) whenever the duties of an officer require him, while within or without the premises of his office, to do or observe something, he has an implied authority, on returning to the official premises, to write down what he did or observed; 2) whenever the duties of an officer require him to obtain information other than personal observation, his return or report is admissible only when he has express authority, by legislative enactment or by executive command, to make it upon such information.[63]

A certificate is a single separate document, not kept in official custody, but made and given out on each occasion to the person applying for it.[64] A certificate is admissible provided: 1) an express authority, by legislative enactment or by executive command, has been given to an officer to prepare and deliver out a certificate of something done or observed by him in his office; 2) the certificate is attached to the document whenever the said certificate concerns an act done to or in some document not retained in the officer's custody, e.g., deed, note, affidavit.[65]

Besides the civil documents mentioned above, there is other written evidence recognized by civil law, a review of which can be very practical for canon law procedure. In conclusion, certain representative items are presented in the following:

A postal-officer's stamp on matter passing through the mail is admissible to evidence the time and place of stamping.[66] For a

---

[60] *Ibidem*, 254.
[61] *Ibidem*, 258.
[62] *Ibidem*, 258.
[63] *Ibidem*, 259.
[64] *Ibidem*, 254.
[65] *Ibidem*, 262.
[66] *Ibidem*, 264.

postmark on an envelope or cover the impress purporting to be the postmark of a government postal officer canceling the mail is sufficiently authenticated[67] to make the postmark admissible.[68] In like manner a reply-letter or a reply-telegram arriving in due course of mail purporting to come in reply to a communication sent to the purporting author is sufficiently authenticated.[69]

A judicial decision or decree inserted in a newspaper by an official authority is sufficiently authenticated.[70]

ART. III. PRIVATE DOCUMENTS

CANON 1813, § 3. Litterae, contractus, testamenta et scripta quaelibet a privatis confecta, privatorum documentorum numero habentur.

In considering the wording of this canon, one must take special notice of the phrase *a privatis confecta.* For from this phrase it can be learned whether or not a letter, contract or will must be evaluated as a public or private instrument. All letters are not private documents. Many are properly public documents. Thus, letters of aggregation to an Archconfraternity,[71] of recommendations (*celebrets*),[72] dimissorial letters,[73] letters attesting the erec-

[67] In Civil Law "a writing or other thing purporting to have been made, sent, authorized, used, or acted on by a specific person, and desired to be offered as such, cannot be received for the purpose of being shown or read to the jury as material or relevent, unless there is also offered some evidence authenticating the person's supposed connection therewith."—Wigmore, 355. Wigmore (*loc. cit.*) commenting upon this principle states that the general mental tendency is to jump to the conclusion without evidence, whenever a corporal object is produced as purporting to be one used or made by a particular person. The mere sight of it in existence seems to prove something. This tendency is especially noticeable with documents. Being a tendency of special danger, the rules of evidence seek to avoid this danger by enforcing the logical necessity of offering some evidence of the supposed connection, before the thing itself is admitted. The specific rules for this purpose concern chiefly documents.

[68] Wigmore, 363.

[69] *Ibidem,* 363.

[70] *Ibidem,* 362.

[71] Canon 723, n. 5.

[72] Canon 804, §§ 1 and 2.

[73] Canon 960.

tion of ecclesiastical associations,[74] remissorial letters authorizing the conduct of the apostolical procedure in the process of the beatification of the Servants of God *per viam non cultus,*[75] testimonial letters for the reception of Holy Orders[76] and the various letters which the law requires in preparation for a person's admission into a religious community[77] must be considered public documents both in view of their purpose and in consideration of the authority from which they emanate. Certainly their purpose is to give public proof concerning a decree issued by the ordinary or by any other public person whose duty it is to issue such decrees. But letters sent by private individuals, or even by public persons for the transaction of some personal or private matter, are private writings.

Likewise contracts and wills when drawn up by a notary are public documents; otherwise they are private documents.[78]

Finally, the canon states that any writings whatsoever which are drawn up by a private person are private documents. To the class of private documents there also pertain those writings which, though they be drawn up by a public person, are nevertheless composed in his capacity of a private person, or which lack the legal formalities which must essentially be present to attach to them a public character.[79] This class of writings includes both those that are signed and those that do not bear a signature. Among the former are included receipts, leases, contracts, acknowledgments of obligations, writings given in testimony of a favor granted, and the like. Among the latter, that is, among private writings which do not bear a signature, are included such items as account-book entries.[80] These entries or annotations are not directly

---

[74] Canon 686, § 5.

[75] Canons 2087, §§ 1 and 3; 2088, § 1; 2089; 2091, § 1; 2093, § 1; etc.

[76] Canon 993.

[77] Canon 544, §§ 2 and 6.

[78] Cf. Lega-Bartoccetti, *Commentarius,* II, 789; Muniz, *Procedimientos Eclesiásticos,* III, n. 370. The civil laws of the respective place must be followed regarding contracts and wills.

[79] Reiffenstuel, *Ius Canonicum Universum,* lib. III, tit. 22, n. 9; Augustine, *Ecclesiastical Trials,* p. 254; Roberti, *De Processibus,* II, n. 367.

[80] Muniz, *Procedimientos Eclesiásticos,* III, n. 370.

intended to give proof in controversies. However, they contain attestations of business transactions which by their very nature have some kind of probative value, which in its force and extent depends upon the degree in which it may rightly be assumed that truth underlies the statements made therein.

The relative strength of the presumption that truthfulness is reflected in these account-book entries is conditioned not only upon the nature of the business transacted, but also upon the status of the person by whom the business was transacted. The probative value attaching to account-book entries which are made in the conduct of a public business wherein books and accounts are regularly kept, for instance, by brokers, merchants, pious institutions, monasteries and other similar religious organizations, is as a rule of considerably greater import than the probative value which attaches to entries that are made by private individuals in connection with the management of their strictly personal or domestic affairs.

CHAPTER VII

The Credibility Attaching to Documents

Art. I. Public Documents

CANON 1814. Documenta publica sive ecclesiastica sive civilia genuina praesumuntur, donec contrarium evidentibus argumentis evincatur.

The canon here clearly distinguishes genuineness from authenticity. For it is evident that by authenticity is meant the external marks of attestation made by a competent person that a certain writing was drawn up in all its parts by him to whom it is attributed. The fact that it can be recognized as a public document necessarily demands that it was drawn up in authentic form by a public person.

A. The Presumption Attaching to Public Documents

The present canon states that public documents, either ecclesiastical or civil, are presumed to be genuine. Moreover, public documents are considered entirely genuine. This means not only that the instrument is presumed to have been executed in all its parts by him to whom such a writing, attestation or allegation is attributed according to the external and legitimate form in which it was drawn up and preserved, but also that the instrument truly and accurately relates the very facts which are set down in writing by such a public person.[1]

This presumption has its foundation in the quality of the person who drew up such a document. For a notary, or any other public person recognized as such by law, who has set down in writing an act executed by him or in his presence is an authoritative or

[1] Roberti, *De Processibus*, II, n. 370; Lega-Bartoccetti, *Commentarius*, II, 791; Muniz, *Procedimientos Eclesiásticos*, III, n. 361: "*Genuino* en el sentido del canon 1814 es el documento que narra hechos verdaderos o contiene disposiciones dadas por aquel a quien se atribuyen."

qualified witness thereto, and gives full credence to the facts in the very manner in which they are related in the instrument.[2]

This presumption of genuineness, however, is a simple presumption of law (*praesumptio iuris*)[3] and as such leaves the way open for proof to the contrary.[4] Thus if anyone is able to prove that faith can not be placed in an instrument, even though it appears to have the marks of a public document, the presumption of genuineness fails and the arguments to the contrary prevail. However, it should be noted that the exception to the presumption can be proved only by evident arguments. For as long as the contrary is not demonstrated by certain evidence the presumption of law stands.[5]

B. The Judicial Challenge Regarding Public Documents.

When a document has been exhibited in court[6] the interested party must be notified, and proper time must be granted him for acquainting himself with the instrument with a view to refuting it if he be able or if he desire to do so; otherwise the trial is invalid.[7] He may take exception[8] to the document by impugning: 1) the efficient cause, inasmuch as the notary or any other official who authenticated the instrument was not legally constituted, did

---

[2] Schmalzgrueber, *Ius Ecclesiasticum Universum,* lib. III, tit. 22, n. 22; De Angelis, *Praelectiones,* tom. IV, pars II, lib. II, tit. 22, art. 1; Lega, *De Iudiciis Ecclesiasticis Civilibus,* I, n. 155; Lega-Bartoccetti, *Commentarius,* II, 791.

[3] Cf. canon 1825.

[4] Canon 1826; Roberti, *De Processibus,* II, n. 325.

[5] Canon 1814.

[6] "Documenta vim probandi in iudicio non habent, nisi originalia sint aut in exemplari authentico exhibita et penes tribunalis cancellariam deposita, exceptis documentis quae publici iuris sunt, ceu leges rite promulgatae."—Canon 1819.

[7] Canon 1861, § 2: "Si novas probationes admittendas censeat, id decernat iudex, audita altera parte, cui congruum tempus concedat ut novas probationes cognoscere et se defendere possit; aliter iudicium nullius est momenti."

[8] "Recognitio aut impugnatio scripturae proponi potest in iudicio tum incidenter, tum ad instar causae principalis."—Canon 1815. It is the right and duty of the judge to decide whether the document shall be recognized as a public instrument or whether the exception shall be sustained.

not act within the scope of his appointment, or was under the stigma of legal infamy (*infamia iuris*) or public excommunication; 2) the material cause, inasmuch as the matter recorded in the document is not true to facts or is disallowed by law; 3) the formal cause, inasmuch as the proper solemnities required by law and custom, such as the affixing of the date, of the seal and of the proper signatures, were not observed when the document was drawn up;[9] 4) the final cause, inasmuch as the document was obtained through force or deceit.[10]

If a public document is contested the burden of proof rests with the one who impugns it. Such proof may be derived from the following sources:

1. The judicial inspection of the document. During this inspection the party who impugns the document may point out the defects contained therein, namely the erasures, corrections, interpolations, discrepancies, etc. It is the right and the duty of the judge to determine the import of such defects.[11] If he feels that he is not adequately qualified to pass competent judgment in this or in any like matter relative to the verity of the documents he should employ the aid of experts.[12] The judge should, furthermore, keep in mind that a defect in a document may be either material or immaterial. It is called material, when it changes the legal effect of the instrument; otherwise it is called immaterial. A written instrument is invalidated by alterations when the following conditions concur: a) if the alteration is material; b) if it was made intentionally; c) if it was made by the grantee or promisee; d) if it was made without the consent of the grantor or promisor; and e) if it was made after the original execution of the instrument.[13]

---

[9] Special notice should be taken of documents which are necessary for the validity or the substance of an act (cf. canons 1017, § 1; 1089, § 1), for if in such cases the document is invalid for lack of some required solemnity, then also the act is invalid and the document is useless for want of something to prove.

[10] Muniz, *Procedimientos Eclesiásticos,* III, n. 377; Reiffenstuel, *Ius Canonicum Universum,* lib. II, tit. 22, n. 256.

[11] Canon 1818.

[12] Cf. canons 1792-1805.

[13] Woywod, *A Practical Commentary on the Code of Canon Law,* II, 287.

2. The presentation of documents of contrary import. If these documents belong to the same litigant they mutually cancel each other; if they are presented by opposing parties they should be compared in order that it may be determined, if that be possible, which of the two is genuine; if this is impossible then the document which is the more worthy of credence is to be followed, namely, the public over the private, the integral over the mutilated, the more recent over the older, due account being taken relative to the circumstances of the case and other elements of proof.[14]

3. The proffering of adverse testimony by witnesses. Naturally, the best witnesses for or against a public document are the documentary witnesses themselves.[15] For if such witnesses deny that they have signed the document, that they have witnessed its execution, or that they have taken the part ascribed to them, or state the facts otherwise than the document gives them, their concordant testimony may overcome the force of the document itself and prove it to have been forged or to be false.[16] Also other than documentary witnesses may be used to prove the truthfulness or falsity of documents.[17] But before extraneous witnesses can prove the falsity of a public instrument, they must have direct knowledge of what they testify. Moreover, the number of the witnesses, their reliability and the certainty of their testimony must be such as to produce conclusive proof.[18] Public documents can not generally be contested or sustained simply by the oath

---

[14] Muniz, *Procedimientos Eclesiásticos,* III, n. 277.

[15] C. 10, X, *de fide instrumentorum,* II, 22.

[16] Pope Innocent III rejected a document when the ones who were alleged to have signed it testified that they knew nothing of the document.—C. 33, X, *de testibus et attestationibus,* II, 20. Cf. Pallottini, *Collectio Resolutionum S. C. Concilii,* X, v. "Instrumentum," n. 6: ". . . si testes contradicunt instrumentum, in quo scripti sunt, praevalent instrumento." The Sacred Roman Rota pronounced a marriage invalid when it was proved that one of the alleged witnesses was not present at the ceremony and that the other did not note the exchange of any signs of consent for the marriage.—S.R.R., *Nullitas matrimonii,* 23 martii, 1914, *coram R.P.D. Guilelmo Sebastianelli,* dec. XII—*Decisiones,* VI (1914), 150-151.

[17] "Probatio per testes in quibuslibet causis admittitur. . . ."—Canon 1754.

[18] Canon 1814; Pirhing, *Jus Canonicum,* lib. II, tit. 20, sec. 1, n. 306.

of one of the parties in the trial.[19] But the legal efficacy inherent in the genuineness, integrity, or authenticity of private documents may be proved by the oath or the confession of one of the parties, if the oath was taken or if the confession was made at a time when no self-interest was at stake and when, as a natural consequence, no ulterior motives could be suspected.[20]

If a doubt arises as to whether a copy has been faithfully transcribed from the original document the judge may, at the instance of the party or of his own accord, decree that the original from which the copy was taken be produced in court in order that the copy may be compared with the original.[21] This comparison is to be made by the judge himself, by the auditor or by a delegate of the judge, in the presence of the notary.[22] The parties have a right to be present when this comparison is made if they so desire. They should, therefore, be notified of the place, the date and the hour at which this comparison is to be made. A copy of this notification and the written results of the comparison, signed by the judge and actuary, should be kept in the acts of the trial.[23]

Muniz[24] indicates a practical mode of procedure for the making of this comparison. When the original and the copy are brought before the judge (or some other person authorized for making the comparison) he will compare the two documents clause by clause, phrase by phrase, word by word, and will order the actuary to note the variance or conformity. If it is impossible or considerably difficult to exhibit the original in court, the judge may delegate an auditor, or request the ordinary of the place where the original document is kept, to inspect and compare the copy with it, and he may also prescribe at what point and how the comparison shall be made.[25] The parties have a right to be present also when this

---

[19] C. 2, X, *de probationibus,* II, 19.
[20] Wernz-Vidal, *Ius Canonicum,* VI, n. 511, p. 457, note 26.
[21] Canon 1821, § 1.
[22] Roberti, *De Processibus,* II, n. 373.
[23] *Loc. cit.;* Muniz, *Procedimientos Eclesiásticos,* III, n. 374.
[24] *Loc. cit.*
[25] Canons 1570 and 1821, § 2.

comparison is made, if they desire to do so. Consequently they must be notified of the time when and of the place where the comparison is to be made. Although canon 1821 does not make mention of the notary as being empowered to make this comparison, when such a comparison is decreed necessary by the judge, it seems safe to say that he may do so, especially in view of the ruling contained in canon 374, § 1, n. 3, as well as in line with the Rotal regulations which provide that the notary may be called on to make this comparison between documents whose identity of form and content is questioned.[26]

As has been stated, if the inherently accredited value of the document has been contested successfully, then the presumption attaching to the public nature of the document fails. However, this does not mean that in every case such a document is not genuine and hence does not retain any legal force and efficacy as a private writing.[27] But if the document has been impugned and proved false in its contents, it is evident that it loses all probative value. A challenge relative to the contents or object of the document is had when one, despite his admission that the document issued from a public person and is therefore public in its character, attempts to prove that the notary did not set down the true

---

[26] "Si questio aut dubium exoriatur, utrum in summariis integre et fideliter referantur documenta, aut in genere utrum exemplaria sint fideliter transcripta, pars interesse habens petitionem Ponenti porriget, ut istorum documentorum a Notario collatio fiat. Notarius, accepto Ponentis rescripto quod recognitionem praescribit, ad collationem procedet et referet de recognitionis exitu, fidem faciens, an documenta sint fideliter in summario relata necne. Haec collatio etiam *ex officio* exigi potest. Rescriptum quo collatio decernitur, et Notarii attestatio de collatione peracta *ad instantiam* partis, alteri parti, si vero *ex officio,* utrique parti, erunt notificanda.

Decretum collationem praescribens est sequens: '*Mandat ut instante NN, fiat collatio documentorum a Notario.*' Attestationis formula: '*Facta collatione documentorum productorum* (vel *scripturarum originalium*) *cum exemplaribus, testor infrascriptus, mihi constare de fidelitate exemplarium cum suis originalibus, NN. Notarius.*' "—*Regulae Servandae in Iudiciis apud Sacrae Romanae Rotae Tribunal,* 4 aug. 1910, § 63, nn. 1, 2—*AAS,* II (1910), 805.

[27] Roberti, *De Processibus,* II, n. 370; Wernz-Vidal, *Ius Canonicum,* VI, n. 511; Coronata, *Institutiones,* n. 1346:—"nisi de actibus agatur in quibus scriptura ad valorem actus ipsius requiritur."

facts in the case. Against the object of a public document no proofs are admitted unless they are direct, that is, they must demonstrate the falsity of the instrument. This direct attack constitutes a judicial suit which is known as the *querela falsi* and may offer the occasion for a criminal trial.[28] Only through the criminal process may a penalty be inflicted for the falsification of documents. If a document has been declared false in a criminal procedure, it is also considered false in relation to contentious suits.[29]

ART. II. PRIVATE DOCUMENTS

Canon 1814 states that public documents are presumed to be genuine, but it is evident that the legal status of private documents is of a different character as regards their credibility. For the presumption of law which favors the genuineness of public documents does not support the private instrument in like fashion. Private instruments, therefore, must be proved to be genuine. This proof of genuineness may be established before or during the process of the trial. During the trial the genuineness of a private document is established either by the acknowledgment of the party that the writing is his own, or by the recognition of the judge whose decision must be reached through the ordinary means of proof. Before the trial it is established by the means recognized by law for the authentication of a private document.[30]

The pre-Code canonists recognized many ways by which a private writing could be authenticated.[31] Today, however, the more common means used for authenticating a private document before the trial are constituted in one or the other of the following ways: 1) that the signature of the document be witnessed or subscribed by a notary or some other public official; 2) that the signature be witnessed or subscribed by two or three private per-

---

[28] Lega, *De Iudiciis Ecclesiasticis Civilibus,* I, n. 457; Roberti, *De Processibus,* II, n. 370; Canons 2360; 2361; 2362; 2406.

[29] Roberti, *De Processibus,* II, n. 370.

[30] Lega-Bartoccetti, *Comentarius,* II, 794.

[31] Cf. Reiffenstuel, *Ius Canonicum Universum,* lib. II, tit. 22, n. 143.

sons who were capable of acting as witnesses; 3) that the document be retained by and preserved in the public archives.

Regarding the first of these means canon 373, § 1, states that not only the notary's writing of, but also his signature on, such a document furnishes for it full faith and credibility. For a notary is a public person, constituted by lawful authority for the purpose of lending full credentials not only to the writings which he himself has executed, but also to the writings which are executed by others if they are attested with his signature.[32] For this reason his signature or written attestation which declares the genuineness of the document gives full credibility. It is to be noted, however, that the attestation covers only the genuineness of the authorship of the writing, unless he witnessed the transaction and attested the truth of the facts recorded in the document.

That witnesses can be used for the purpose of proving the genuineness of a writing must be admitted from canon 1754, which states that proof through witnesses can be admitted in any case. It is to be understood that documentary witnesses provide the best means of proving the genuineness of the document, for it was just for this purpose that they witnessed and subscribed their names to the act in the drawing up of the instrument. However, other than documentary witnesses may be admitted for proving the genuineness of a writing, provided that they have knowledge of what they testify.[33]

Before the promulgation of the Code it was the common teaching of the canonists[34] and the usual practice of the courts[35] to attribute full credibility to private documents which were preserved in public archives and which were declared authentic by the custodian of the archives, because they obtained this recognition from

---

[32] Lega, *De Iudiciis Ecclesiasticis Civilibus,* I, n. 152; Noval, *De Iudiciis,* n. 142.

[33] Canon 1754. Cf. also Lega-Bartoccetti, *Commentarius,* II, 795.

[34] Reiffenstuel, *Ius Canonicum Universum,* lib. II, tit. 22, n. 108; Schmalgzueber, *Ius Ecclesiasticum Universum,* lib. III, tit. 22, n. 40; Pirhing, *Jus Canonicum,* lib. II, tit. 22, n. 30.

[35] *S.R.R., Decisiones Recentiores,* Par. V, dec. 45 (1627), n. 1 sq.; Par. VIII, dec. 3 (1638), n. 12.

the presumption of law. In consequence such documents were held equal to those which had been authenticated by a notary.

According to the teaching of Lega-Bartoccetti the same principle holds in the Code. For, as they state,[36] the Code extends to the universal Church what was prescribed for Italy alone on April 29, 1578 [April 27, 1587],[37] by Pope Sixtus V. On June 14, 1727, Pope Benedict XIII in his Constitution *Maxima Diligentia* [*Maxima Vigilantia*][38] determined with more exactness the prescriptions of Sixtus V. It is, moreover, the precept of the Code that public archives are to be erected in every diocesan curia, and that these archives are to be entrusted to the care of the chancellor under the special vigilance of the ordinary.[39]

It is evident from the wording of canon 375, § 1, *"instrumenta et scripturae, quae negotia diocesana tum spiritualia tum temporalia spectant,"* that not only public but private writings as well are to be admitted into the public diocesan archives. The presumption of genuineness for the private documents preserved in public archives is based on the assumed fact that the chancellor, who is a notary by virtue of his office, would not have admitted the document unless he had recognized it as being genuine. Wherefore Lega-Bartoccetti conclude that the documents preserved in the diocesan archives and declared as authentic by the chancellor according to the prescribed rules must be accepted as having complete trustworthiness everywhere and as meriting full credence from all.[40]

This presumption is a simple presumption of law. In virtue of canon 1828 it admits both direct and indirect proofs to the contrary. If, therefore, it is shown that the archives are carelessly kept and the prescribed rules are not observed, then the authenti-

---

[36] *Commentarius,* II, p. 796, note 2.

[37] Cf. *Bullarium Romanum* (25 vols., Augustae Taurinorum, 1857-1872), VIII, 840.

[38] Cf. *Ibidem,* XXII, 560.

[39] Canons 375-382.

[40] *Commentarius,* II, p. 796, note 1: "Doctores et iurisprudentia limitant valorem scripturarum extractarum a publico archivo, tantum inter subditos; quia supponitur archivi auctoritas et officiales custodes derivari ab Ordinario loci, sed hanc opinionem esse parum probabilem patet ex dictis."

cated character of the private documents taken from them should not be recognized, and their status should rather be regarded as the equivalent of that of simple private instruments, inasmuch as the presumption of law can not be applied in their behalf.

Since all the conditions which are requisite in order that credibility will attach to the documents which are drawn from the public archives are also found stated in the law regarding the keeping of the documents preserved in the parochial archives,[41] canon 384, § 1, places these latter documents on a basis of juridical equality with those which are preserved in the episcopal archives. But since the purpose of the parochial archives is the preservation of those books which are properly parochial in character,[42] the other books, especially the account books, have no more value than other private documents.

Private archives, or those which do not measure up to the requirements of law concerning their erection, their custodianship, and episcopal visitation and inspection, do not lend themselves to the establishing of the legal presumption of genuineness for the private instruments contained therein. Private documents taken from them, therefore, are not to be considered as authenticated. However, inasmuch as some archives, although they be private, are kept with special diligence, they may give rise to more or less weighty presumptions (*praesumptiones hominis*).[43]

---

[41] Erection by public authority; pastor as legitimate custodian; subjection to the visitation and special inspection of the ordinary. Cf. canon 470. Cf. also S. C. de Prop. Fide, instr. a. 1883, n. 32: "Ac proinde locorum Ordinarii sedulo curabunt ut libri baptizatorum, confirmatorum, et matrimonio copulatorum, nec non defunctorum a parochis diligentissime exarentur et accurate custodiantur."—*Fontes,* n. 4901.

[42] Canon 470, § 1.

[43] After the fashion of a legal presumption, so also the presumption invoked by a judge may belong to one or the other of the three recognized classes: It may be 1) *levis;* 2) *gravis;* 3) *violenta* or *gravissima.*

CHAPTER VIII

Probative Force of Documents

Art. I. Public Ecclesiastical Documents

CANON 1816. Documenta publica fidem faciunt de iis quae directe et principaliter in eisdem affirmantur.

In the preceding chapter it was shown that the law presumes public documents to have emanated from public officials and that these public officials have set down in such documents the true facts in the case. Upon this presumption of genuineness the force of legal proof is founded. It is for the common good, namely, the settlement of contested rights and the certification of juridical facts, that the law determines such value for these documents.[1]

Inasmuch as public documents furnish a special assurance of genuineness, not only as to their authorship but also as to the truth of the facts recorded therein, it logically follows that such documents have the distinctive capacity of providing full or complete proof in court concerning the object of the instrument.[2] For, whenever an official has drawn up in written form his own act or what the contracting parties agreed to in his presence, he as a qualified witness gives public credibility to the facts he relates in such written instruments. As a result such instruments affect not only the contracting parties among themselves, but also those who are not parties to the contract. However, public instruments do not exert their full probative value against the contractants and

---

[1] Roberti, *De Processibus,* II, n. 370.

[2] "Probatio plena ita definire solet, quod illa fit, quae tantam fidem faciat, quantum ad finiendam controversiam sufficiat."—Mascardus, *Conclusiones Omnium Probationum,* I, q. IV, n. 15; cf. Whalen, *The Value of Testimonial Evidence in Matrimonial Procedure,* The Catholic University of America Canon Law Studies, n. 99 (Washington, D. C.: The Catholic University of America, 1935), p. 56.

outsiders alike. In order that this truth may the better be understood, a distinction must be made between the recording or the written attestation of a contract, fact, or transaction on the one hand, and the juridical force of the act itself on the other.[3]

A common example is found in the case of a document which is drawn up by the pastor in the proper parochial books in which he records a marriage. Such a document establishes full credibility, and therefore furnishes full factual proof of the contracting of a matrimonial union. If, however, at some future date a question arises concerning the validity of the marriage in view of some attendant diriment impediment, then such a document does not serve to prove the validity of the marriage but only the fact of its canonical celebration. This is true of any public document both ecclesiastical and civil.[4] Hence, when it is said that public documents exert their full value of proof against outsiders or third parties, it is to be understood that these can not deny the trust and assurance which attaches to the recorded act, even though they are not parties thereto, and even though it would be to the latter's advantage to break the contract. Such a case would obtain in the matter of a public document which records the sale of an object that did not belong to the seller. After the sale was completed and possession of the object was obtained, prescription begins in favor of the buyer. After the required time elapses, all other requirements having been fulfilled, the object is prescribed against its true owner, who can not oppose the sale by denying the validity of the act for which the public document gives its assurance, although he himself was not a party to the contract. Wherefore, it is true that a public instrument has full probative value against those who are not parties to the contract. However, it is equally true that the agreement which the contracting parties make between themselves can not directly or in virtue of the contract either profit or harm outsiders. It is evident, however, that the heirs and also those who hold vested interests with one of the contesting parties are not to be considered as outsiders, but

---

[3] Lega-Bartoccetti, *Commentarius,* II, 791.

[4] *Loc. cit.*

stand identified in their eventual loss or gain with him in whose interests they share.[5]

The law does not intend that even public documents should furnish full proof in all their parts. Thus canon 1816 states the definite and practical principle that public documents afford assurance (*fidem faciunt*)[6] relative to such facts as are asserted in them without subordination to (*directe*), and free of all dependence on (*principaliter*) prior or primary issues.[7] This is to say that the facts to which such a direct and independent expression is given in public documents are so evidenced that the judge is liberated from seeking further proof. In fact, they furnish the moral certitude, as required by canon 1869, § 1, with such conclusiveness that no further choice is left him,[8] and no added corroboration is to be sought.[9]

It is important, therefore, that the judge determine which facts are thus asserted, before he will be able to estimate properly the probative value of any document. Directly or independently affirmed are those facts whose recording answers to the substantial and primary purpose of the instrument. Facts are affirmed but indirectly when they relate something in a merely discursive

---

[5] Lega-Bartoccetti, *Commentarius,* II, 792: ". . . verum aeque est rem seu conventionem *inter alios actam aliis nempe extraneis, neque nocere prodesse posse; nempe directe et vi ipsius conventionis.* At non censentur extranei qui sunt haeredes aut causam habentes ab uno ex contradicentibus et planum est."

[6] "Fides hic idem est ac valor probatorius in iudicio ecclesiastico."—Wernz-Vidal, *Ius Canonicum,* VI, n. 511. The distinction between *fides* and proof is explained by Wernz-Vidal as follows:—"Epistola privata fidem meretur sc. quod is qui epistolam scripsit haec vel illa dixit aut narravit; sed valorem iuridicum probandi quod in epistola asseritur non habet, nisi forte contra asserentem."—*Ibidem,* note 22.

[7] Cf. S.R.R., *Nullitas matrimonii,* 23 iulii, 1918, *coram R.P.D. Seraphino Many,* dec. X—*Decisiones,* X (1918), 83; *AAS,* XI (1919), 158.

[8] S.C.de Prop. Fide, instr. a. 1883, § 32—*Fontes,* n. 4901; *ASS,* XVIII (1885), 369. This Instruction was addressed to the bishops of the United States and is, with few exceptions, identical with the one addressed to the bishops of the Oriental Church in 1883 by the Sacred Congregation of the Holy Office.—S.C.S. Off., instr. (ad Ep. Rituum Orient.), a. 1883, n. 32—*Fontes,* n. 1076.

[9] C. 2, X, *de probationibus.* II, 19; Reg. 31, R.J., in VI°.

or narrative fashion, unless of course that very discourse or narration of facts forms a necessary part of the substantial intent of the document. And facts are affirmed in a merely accessory manner when they do not serve the primary and immediate purpose inherent in the document. Hence any facts which are merely incidentally and accessorily affirmed are not included among those parts of a public document which furnish full probative value.[10] The mention of these incidental and accessory facts, nevertheless, gives rise to a favorable presumption (*praesumptio hominis*) and a probable conjecture relative to their truth. They may, when discreetly joined with other signs, warrants, and indications, approximate the value of proof.[11]

From the above it can be seen that a baptismal record fully proves only the fact of the baptism conferred upon the individual named, the date of the baptism, the identity of the god-parents, and also that of the minister who conferred the sacrament. The marriage record likewise is conclusive proof only that the parties named gave the external matrimonial consent, that the marriage ceremony took place on the recorded date and that the persons named as witnesses assisted in that capacity. But the accessory information, such as that of the date of birth,[12] of the qualities and

---

[10] Noval, *De Iudiciis*, n. 550; Roberti, *De Processibus*, II, n. 370:—"a) *directe* affirmantur ea quae publica persona potuit sensibus percipere, et quibus ipsa valet addere publicam fidem. Ita, e.g., si partes coram notario declarent se stipulasse contractum, publica fides declarationi, non autem contractui adiicitur. Item si notarius declaret quempiam morbo mentis laborare, declaratio nonnisi speciem externam afficit; notarius enim non valet de morbis mentis iudicare. b) *principaliter* asseruntur eo quae spectat authentica declaratio. Quae incidenter proferuntur non habent plenam fidem, sed arbitrio iudicis aestimantur." Cf. also Cappello, *Summa Iuris Canonici*, III, n. 281.

[11] Coronata, *Institutiones*, n. 1347; Muniz, *Procedimientos Eclesiásticos*, III, n. 378; S.R.R., *Nullitas matrimonii*, 28 aug., 1911, *coram R.P.D. Aloysio Sincero*, dec. XXXIX—*Decisiones*, III (1911), 441; S.R.R., *Nullitas matrimonii*, 9 iulii, 1918, *coram R.P.D. Seraphino Many*, dec. X—*Decisiones*, X (1918), 83; S.C.C., *Pisauren.*, 28 apr., 16 iun. 1781—*Fontes*, n. 3815.

[12] In the civil law "the fact of birth may be proved . . . by a registry of baptism . . . but a mere registry of baptism is not, as an official registry of birth may be, evidence of the date, though stated in it, further than to show that it must have been prior to the date recorded as that of baptism,

conditions of the persons or of their domiciles, is not fully proved by the fact of its being recorded in such public registers.[13]

Both from the fact that the date of birth can not be fully proved from baptismal certificates, and from the well known fact that not all civil governments keep vital statistics, there arises, no doubt, a reason for the exclusion of the impediment of non-age in the list of those matrimonial impediments for whose existence proof can be established according to the ruling of canon 1990 by means of a simplified procedure apart from the full judicial procedure that attends a formal trial in the ecclesiastical courts. It is not entirely clear however, as Wanenmacher observes,[14] whether the cases of non-age must always be tried within the complete judicial framework of a formal trial. For in some cases of non-age there may exist such notorious facts that in them the element of notoriety supplants all need of further proof.[15] Whether or not this notoriety makes it any longer necessary in such cases to employ successively the various judicial functions that attend a formal trial from its inception to its close is a matter in which, according to the doctrine of many authors, the Code has not spoken a final and definitive word. But in view of the abiding general principle in the law of the Church, namely, that the laws which are enacted as a safeguard against a general danger nevertheless continue in their binding force even when in some particular case no danger is present,[16] as well as in consideration of the fact that canon 1990 sets up an all-inclusive list of the cases for which a simplified mode of procedure apart from a formal

---

. . . unless the statement of the time of birth is shown to have been made by direction of a member of the family since deceased, so as to bring it within the rule admitting declarations as to facts of pedigree."—Abbot, *Trial Evidence* (New York, 1813), p. 111.

[13] S.R.R., *Nullitas matrimonii*, 4 martii, 1916, *coram R.P.D. Ioseph Mori*, dec. VI—*Decisiones*, VIII (1916), 71; *AAS*, VIII (1916), 372.

[14] *Canonical Evidence in Marriage Cases*, nn. 9 and 45.

[15] "*Non indigent probatione facta notoria, ad norman can.* 2197, nn. 2, 3."—Canon 1747, 1o. Cf. also the doctrine of Pirhing, *Ius Canonicum*, lib. II, tit. 19, cap. 4, n. 31.

[16] Canon 21.

trial is now made admissible,[17] it appears to the present writer that proof concerning the existence of the impediment of non-age must be sought by employing all the formalities of the ordinary judicial procedure outlined in canons 1960-1989 and articles 1-225 of the Instruction of the Congregation of the Discipline of the Sacraments issued on August 15, 1936.

In like manner the account contained in the baptismal register does not afford proof of the legitimacy of the baptized child simply in view of the names of its alleged parents in the acknowledged relationship of husband and wife. Such an account does not furnish proof of the child's legitimacy even when it expressly states that the child is the legitimate offspring of its parents. It must however be noted that, even though the account of the parents' relationship of husband and wife and the explicit mention of the child's legitimacy do not form part of the direct and primary statement of the baptismal register, and correspondingly fall short of offering full proof for the child's juridical status of legitimacy, yet they establish the favorable presumption of legitimacy to such an extent, that the presumption can be rebutted only by strict proof to the contrary.

For the same reason a baptismal entry which notes the fact of illegitimacy is not of itself sufficient proof to rebut the contrary presumption if the child's mother was married,[18] or if the child in question has been in quasi-possession of a legitimate name. In certain cases of this kind the Sacred Congregation of the Council has ordered the registers corrected.[19]

If a baptismal register or an attestation issued from it contains

---

[17] Bouscaren, *The Canon Law Digest* (2 vols. and Supplement, 1934, 1937 and 1941, Milwaukee), Supplement, p. 194.

[18] Cf. canon 1115; Gasparri, *Tractatus Canonicus de Matrimonio* (2 vols., Romae: Typis Polyglottis Vaticanis, 1932), n. 1113.

[19] "Unde legitimus renunciari debet, nec aliqua indiget dispensatione, qui descriptus inventus est in libro Baptizatorum Filius certae Mulieris, sed ex incerto Patre, communiter tamen Filius legitimus dictae Mulieris et certi Viri ab omnibus creditus, adeoque dictus liber Baptizatorum est corrigendus *in Tudertina Legitimitatis*, die 16 ianuarii, 1717."—Pallottini, *Collectio Resolutionum S. C. Concilii*, XIII, v. "Matrimonium," n. 26. For another case of similar import cf. S.C.C., *Verulana*, 9 aug. 1884—*Fontes*, n. 4264.

the annotation of a marriage subsequently entered into by the baptized person, this annotation is not to be considered as a direct or primary statement of the baptismal register, and does not therefore beget full proof. Hence no marriage may be declared invalid on the score of a pre-existing bond or in view of the impediment of affinity ensuing therefrom simply by reason of the mention that is made of them in such an annotation. Nevertheless the annotation affords so strong a presumption of the previous marriage and of the impediment of affinity that a new marriage is permitted only when it has been demonstrated that the recorded marriage has been dissolved and that a dispensation from the impediment has been obtained, or that the recorded entry does not correspond to fact and reality.[20]

The statement in the record of baptism that the non-Catholic parents requested or consented to the Catholic baptism of the child, and furnished guarantees for the Catholic rearing of the child, is not a primary statement in the baptismal entry, but it is generally the only evidence available and is decisive of the fact that the child was aggregated to the Catholic Church and thus through its Catholic baptism became subject to the law of the Church regarding the impediment of disparity of cult according to canon 1070, § 1.[21]

What has been said of parochial records applies equally and even to a greater degree to curial registers. Thus the curial registers of Sacred Ordinations, of dispensations, of secret marriages and of other acts of a like nature give conclusive proof that the recorded act has been performed.

In cases relative to the Pauline privilege, the making of the interpellations and the grant which dispensed from making them are ordinarily proved from the original documents of the interpellations and of the granted dispensation, but normally sufficient evidence may be derived from the annotations contained in the parochial register or in the curial records, even though their annotations can not be considered as reflecting a statement of primary and direct import relative to the recorded fact of marriage.[22]

---

[20] Wanenmacher, *Canonical Evidence in Marriage Cases,* n. 371.

[21] *Loc. cit.*

[22] S.C.S. Off., instr. (ad Ep. Rituum Orient.), a. 1883, § 45—*Fontes,* n. 1076. Cf. also S.C. de Prop. Fide, instr. a. 1883, § 45—*Fontes,* n. 4901.

Any statement contained in the record of the judicial acts written and authenticated[23] by the chancellor or by other notaries of the court[24] is considered as part of the direct and primary content of the document. However, a distinction must be made between what the notary attests and what the witnesses testify, for the acts thus recorded beget full proof that the witness spoke as the notary has attested, but they do not by his attestation beget conclusive proof that the testimony of the witnesses is true.[25]

Just as the mention of accessory facts, so the absence of some annotation of a fact which by law or custom should be found in such documents, gives rise to a presumption, more or less grave according to the circumstances, of the non-existence of that fact. Thus, if the baptismal certificate which is presented for the purpose of indicating the free state requisite for the contracting of matrimony contains no annotation of a previous contracted marriage, there arises a presumption that the person whose name is recorded has not, at least *in facie ecclesiae,* contracted such a marriage. This presumption obtains as a general rule despite the occasional evidence of neglect or failure on the part of some pastors who do not scrupulously follow out the demand of ecclesiastical law to record all duly reported marriages in the baptismal register.[26]

In like manner there arises a presumption that no dispensation was granted if no mention of a dispensation is found in the marriage register.[27]

The same degree of negative presumption does not arise, how-

---

[23] Cf. canon 1643, § 1.

[24] Cf. canons 372; 374; 1585.

[25] Wanenmacher, *Canonical Evidence in Marriage Cases,* n. 373.

[26] Canon 1103, § 2: "Praeterea, ad normam can. 470, § 2, parochus in libro quoque baptizatorum adnotet coniugem tali die in sua paroecia matrimonium contraxisse. Quod si coniux alibi baptizatus fuerit, matrimonii parochus notitiam initi contractus ad parochum baptismi sive per se sive per curiam episcopalem transmittat, ut matrimonium in baptizatorum librum referatur." Cf. also canons 1011; 576, § 2.

[27] S.R.R., *Nullitas matrimonii,* 31 martii, 1909, *coram R.P.D. Seraphino Many,* dec. III—*Decisiones,* I (1909), 27; S.R.R., *Nullitas matrimonii,* 2 aug., 1913, *coram R.P.D. Antonio Perathoner,* dec. XLIII—*Decisiones,* V (1913), 506.

ever, when there is no mention or annotation in the marriage register of the proper delegation given to a priest who had no ordinary power to assist at marriages in the parish where the marriage was contracted. The absence of any annotation to that effect does not afford a grave presumption that the assisting priest performed the marriage without the necessary delegation. Both the congregation of the Council and the Sacred Roman Rota have, in such cases, ascribed the absence of any annotation to inadvertence, forgetfulness, or neglect on the part of the pastor rather than to the lack of any granted delegation. Any slight presumption which may arise because of the absence of any mention of delegation is easily and sufficiently rebutted by some favorable circumstance arising out of the consideration of person, of place, of time, of custom, or of other attendant factors.[28]

The curial registers of dispensations give conclusive proof of the granting of the dispensations, but they do not give full proof of the actual existence of the impediment from which the dispensation was granted. Wanenmacher[29] relates the case of a man who had posed as a Catholic at his first wedding, and then in attempting a second marriage with a Catholic girl posed as a non-baptized person. When the first marriage was later contested on the grounds of disparity of cult, the entry of the second marriage in the curial marriage register with the annotation that the man professed no religion, and that a dispensation from the impediment of disparity of cult had been granted, was brought into evidence. But this entry did not give full proof of the existence of the impediment; it simply established a presumption that the man had not been baptized. This presumption together with positive evidence was accepted by the Holy Office as proof of his non-baptism.

In cases wherein no annotation is discovered both in the parochial and in the curial registers, the presumption amounts

---

[28] S.C.C., *in Theatina*, 16 martii, 1771,—Pallottini, *Collectio Resolutionum S. C. Concilii*, XIII, v. "Matrimonium," n. 22; S.R.R., *Nullitas matrimonii*, 23 iul. 1918, *coram R.P.D. Seraphino Many*, dec. X—*Decisiones*, X (1918), 83-84. Cf. also *AAS*, XIV (1922), 527.

[29] *Canonical Evidence in Marriage Cases*, n. 372. The author there cites an unpublished decision of the Holy Office given on March 18, 1913, Num. Protoc. 1709./1929.

to a moral certainty.[30] This moral certitude is sufficient to permit the ordinary to proceed with a declaration of nullity even in the extraordinary procedure delineated in canon 1990.[31]

It is scarcely necessary to note that any conclusive proof that the dispensation was granted, such as may be furnished by the testimony of competent witnesses, rebuts such a presumption and destroys all the moral certitude that may previously have followed from it. But, in comparison with the case just mentioned, much stronger proof to the contrary is required to rebut the current presumption, namely, that no dispensation has been granted, when indeed mention is made in the register of the granting of a dispensation from one of the existent impediments, but no mention occurs of the additional impediment which was known to exist,[32] or when an annotation is made of the granted dispensation relative to the impediment of simple consanguinity, although in fact the relationship was multiple.[33]

The absence of any annotation in both the curial and the parochial registers to the effect that in a Pauline privilege case the interpellations were made, or that a dispensation warranted their omission, gives rise to a legal presumption that the inter-

---

[30] S.R.R., *Nullitas matrimonii,* 20 maii, 1910, *coram R.P.D. Aloysio Sincero,* dec. XVIII—*Decisiones,* II (1910), 166.

[31] Vermeersch-Creusen, *Epitome Iuris Canonici,* III, n. 297:—"Certitudo de non concessa dispensatione omni modo legitimo praeberi potest, dummodo extra controversiam versetur." When the Pontifical Commission for the Authentic Interpretation of the Canons of the Code was asked whether the "equal certitude" mentioned in canon 1990 can be had from some other legitimate source besides a certain and authentic document, it answered in the affirmative to this question on June 16, 1931—*AAS,* XXIII (1931), 353. It should here be added however that the judge must bear in mind the possibility of the fact that in the interim a dispensation was granted from the existing bond if the marriage was never consummated, or that a dispensation was employed to remove the impediments of consanguinity, of affinity, or of *crimen,* as noted in the Constitution *Altitudo* of Pope Paul III, June 1, 1537 (*C.I.C. Documenta,* VI) and canon 1053 of the Code.

[32] Cf. canon 1077; S.R.R., *Nullitas matrimonii,* 31 martii, 1909, *coram R.P.D. Seraphino Many,* dec. III—*Decisiones,* I (1909), 27.

[33] S.R.R., *Nullitas matrimonii,* 12 ianuarii, 1921, *coram R.P.D. Raphael Chimenti,* dec. I—*Decisiones,* XIII (1921), 12.

pellations were not made or that the dispensation requisite to warrant their omission was never granted.[84]

ARTICLE II. PUBLIC CIVIL DOCUMENTS

Pre-Code legislation regarding the probative value of public civil documents was somewhat indefinite. As has been noted before, Innocent III wrote that documents issuing from the King of Scotland might be relied upon in the diocesan courts, if it was the custom in that country to hold such writings as authentic for the ecclesiastical courts.[85]

In 1868 the Holy Office, in outlining the procedure that had to be followed in the proof of death in order to establish the free state of the surviving party wishing to enter a second marriage, prescribed that, in case a certificate of death could not be obtained from ecclesiastical sources, the records of the civil authority, with due precautions, might be employed for that purpose.[86]

Later, in 1883, both the Sacred Congregation of the Propagation of the Faith and the Congregation of the Holy Office, in an Instruction addressed to the bishops of the United States and the Oriental Church respectively, attributed merely extrajudicial value to public civil documents.[87] On some particular occasions, however, an exception was granted to the effect that full faith might be placed in public civil documents.[88]

---

[84] S.C.S. Off., instr. (ad Ep. Rituum Orient.) a. 1883, n. 45—*Fontes*, n. 1076.

[85] C. 9, X, *de fide instrumentorum*, II, 22.

[86] "Hinc ad praescriptum eorumdem sacrorum Canonum, documentum authenticum obitus diligenti studio exquiri omnino debet; exaratum scilicet ex regestis paroeciae, vel xenedochii, vel militiae, vel etiam, si haberi nequeat ab auctoritate ecclesiastica, a gubernio civili loci in quo, ut supponitur, persona obierit."—S.C.S. Off., instr. 13 maii 1868, n. 2—*Fontes* 1002.

[87] "Quamvis documenta vel a sola civili potestate, . . . vim habere possint aliquando ad factum de matrimonio celebrato extraiudicialiter confirmandum, . . ."—S.C. de Prop. Fide, instr. a. 1883, n. 33—*Fontes*, n. 4901; S.C.S. Off., instr. (ad Ep. Rituum Orient.), a. 1883, n. 33.—*Fontes*, n. 1076.

[88] Cf., e.g., S.C.C., *Leopolien*, 15 dec., 1877, 23 mart. 1878—*Fontes*, n. 4239; Bassibey, *Le Mariage* (Paris: Libraire Religieuse H. Oudin, 1899), n. 466.

The Code awards the same probative force, in principle, to both civil and ecclesiastical public documents. For, like the latter, civil documents are presumed to be genuine,[39] and therefore prove the facts which are directly and primarily affirmed in them.[40] However, this principle can not always be accepted and applied on its face value. For there are circumstances in which the primary statements in civil public documents can not be accepted in an ecclesiastical court as furnishing complete proof. An example illustrating this fact took place in connection with the earthquake in Sicily and Calabria, December 28, 1908, when the Holy See declined to accept the certificates of death issued by the Italian government, on the ground that they were mere declarations of death based on the fact that the individuals were missing after the disaster.[41]

Rice,[42] with reference to the Church's attitude towards the civil declaration of death,[43] states that there are two extremes to be avoided.

In the first place, the author observes, the civil declaration of death cannot be accepted by the ecclesiastical authorities as full proof of death.[44] For the primary purpose of the State in declaring a missing person dead is different from that of the Church. The Church is first of all intent upon protecting the unity and indissolubility of marriage; the State is only secondarily interested

---

[39] Canon 1814.

[40] Canon 1816.

[41] S.C. de Sacr., 12 mart. 1910—*AAS,* II (1910), 196.

[42] *Proof of Death in Pre-Nuptial Investigation,* The Catholic University of America, Canon Law Studies, n. 123 (Washington, D. C.: The Catholic University of America Press, 1940), p. 65.

[43] Although the author is treating expressly of a written declaration by the civil authorities of the death of missing persons, his teaching will be helpful in estimating the value of any document issued by the civil authority.

[44] Here Rice quotes a response to a query presented by the Vicar Apostolic of Pondicherry, India. "Hinc quaeritur: 1. Utrum provisiones legis civilis de absentibus coniugibus, locum certitudinis moralis de eorum morte tenere possint, ac consequenter utrum derelicti coniuges, perfectis et impletis istis provisionibus, aliud matrimonium legitime contrahere valeant. . . . R. 1. Iuxta expositum, Negative, et expendendos esse casus particulares ab ipso Vic. Ap. iuxta Instructionem quae eidem communicetur."—S.C.S. Off. (Pondicherry), 28 iun. 1865—*Fontes,* n. 984.

in the question from the standpoint of marriage; its primary interest is in the economic side of the problem, especially with regard to disposal of the missing person's property. The State places much emphasis on the lapse of the statutory period; this is of importance for the Church only as one of the corroborating circumstances which lead to moral certainty of the death of the person. In such cases merely to rely on the result of the civil investigation is to expose the sacrament of matrimony to the danger of abuse.

On the other hand, continues Rice, the civil declaration of death can prove of great value to the ecclesiastical authorities, and should be taken into consideration by the ordinary in arriving at a decision on the question.[45] It must not be forgotten that the civil authorities have at their disposal much greater means than the Church for obtaining certainty of the death of a person—the police, missing persons' bureau, official records of various kinds. At least the grounds should be considered upon which the civil officials arrived at their decision, and it will be for the ordinary to decide whether he believes that this provides a basis for compelling proof.

Affidavits are frequently resorted to as a means of documentary proof or evidence in English-speaking countries. These affidavits are written declarations or statements confirmed either by oath or by a solemn affirmation. Since they are oftentimes presented in ecclesiastical courts, the judge should be careful not to ascribe to them more probative force than they purport to carry. An affidavit merely certifies that a specific person made a solemn affirmation confirmed by oath before a duly qualified notary public at a certain time. Obviously, such a statement in itself, even though it was made under oath, does not constitute full proof in every litigation.

---

[45] "Argumenta etiam desumi possunt ex actis a Tribunali civili confectis et deinde super illis, instituto examine, ubi nihil contrarium reperiatur, ab Ecclesiastica potestate, ferri debet sententia, qua declaratur satis constare de obitu personae de cuius existentia inquiritur."—S.C.S. Off., 6 febr. 1861 (1863)—quoted in S.C.S. Off., 8 maii 1891 (date here is given as 1863)—*Fontes,* n. 1135, and in S. C. de Sacr., 16 dec. 1910 (date here is given as 1861)—*Fontes,* n, 2104.

According to the opinion of the Sacred Roman Rota, declarations and affirmations contained in affidavits do not constitute full proof in ecclesiastical courts, since they are not considered as judicial depositions in Canon Law. They do, however, give corroborative force to extant proof. Moreover, since they are public documents they constitute surety about those things which are directly and primarily affirmed.[46]

The 1936 Instruction of the Sacred Congregation of the Sacraments, in dealing with matrimonial procedure in diocesan tribunals, rules that if a doubt or exception is concerned with the truth of a document, an incidental question should be proposed even *ex officio,* and all those who are presumed to know anything about the origin or truth of the document are to be summoned and examined judicially.[47] Doheny,[48] in commenting on article 162, § 2, of the said Instruction, remarks that, whenever the truth of a document known in English and American law as an affidavit is called into question, the matter should be settled by introducing an incidental question. For instance, an affidavit might affirm that a certain person appeared before a Notary Public on a certain day in the presence of certain witnesses and attested to certain facts. The mere affidavit would not of itself establish the truth of the facts asserted, particularly if these statements were made by one of the consorts impugning the validity of the marriage. Hence, there would be need of a judicial examination to ascertain the inherent truth of the assertion.

---

[46] "Depositiones coram iudice ecclesiastico factae plene confirmantur ab iis quae coram notario civili sub iuramento declaraverunt. Hae declarationes enim, etsi perfectam probationem efficere nequeant, cum non constituant iudiciales testificationes iuxta can. 1754 et seqq., eoque magis quod in iis conficiendis defuerat vinculi defensor, cuius praesentia requiritur ad normam canonis 1587, valorem tamen adminiculativum habent. Prout enim a notario publico rite confectae fuerunt secundum Statuum Foederatorum Americae Septentrionalis leges, documenta publica constituunt, ideoque ex can. 1816 'fidem faciunt de iis quae directe et principaliter in eisdem affirmantur.' "—S.R.R., *Nullitas matrimonii,* 5 iunii, 1926, *coram R.P.D. Josepho Florczak,* dec. XXIV, n. 7—*Decisiones,* XVIII (1926), 195.

[47] S.C.S., instr., 15 aug., 1936, article 162, n. 2—*AAS,* XXVIII (1936), 313-361, and in particular p. 345.

[48] *Canonical Procedure in Matrimonial Cases* (Milwaukee: Bruce, 1938), p. 282.

There is likewise a limitation placed against judicial papers emanating from the civil courts. Such judicial papers are indeed public documents, but they are admitted in ecclesiastical courts as proof of only such facts as lie within the civil competency for adjudication, e.g., insanity or guilt in giving the reasons for a civil divorce. Hence, to the end that the petitioner be either exonerated from or charged with the cause that led to the disruption of the marriage, an authentic copy of the findings of the court in granting the divorce decree must be sent on with the acts in all cases wherein a dissolution of the natural bond of marriage is sought in favor of the Faith of the newly converted party.[49] Such a document should also accompany the acts which were drawn up with the view of seeking a dispensation from a ratified-unconsummated marriage.

It naturally follows that in those matters wherein the civil courts have no competence, which is verified, for instance, when they declare marriages between Christians invalid, even the primary content of such a decision has no value in the ecclesiastical courts. It goes without saying that the same rule applies regarding the decisions handed down by non-Catholic church courts.[50]

The general practice of diocesan courts which requires a civil divorce certificate in cases of declaration of nullity, or in cases wherein the use of the Pauline privilege is granted, is not indeed demanded by the Code, but is a wise procedure which should be followed to avoid conflict with the civil law.

The Instruction of the Sacred Congregation of the Propagation of the Faith, which has been frequently quoted above, by the very fact of determining the value of documents issued by non-Catholic churches admitted their use in the ecclesiastical courts. But this Congregation attributed merely extrajudicial value to such documents.[51] Consequently they constitute proof only in the quality and with the limitations of private documents. Yet,

---

[49] Wanenmacher, *Canonical Evidence in Marriage Cases,* n. 345.

[50] Cf. S.C. de Prop. Fide, instr. a. 1883, n. 44—*Fontes,* n. 4901.

[51] *Ibidem,* n. 33:—"Quamvis documenta . . . ab haereticis manantia, vim habere possint aliquando ad factum de matrimonio celebrato extraiudicialiter confirmandum, . . ."

as Wanenmacher[52] observes, they frequently furnish the only proof to be had of a death, of a marriage, or of a baptism. Baptism records of heretical churches are frequently required and accepted in the quality of full proof of the baptism bestowed, namely, when the judge may properly believe that they are genuine and credible, or if there are other supporting circumstances pointing to the likelihood that the recorded baptism was actually conferred.[53]

ARTICLE III. PRIVATE DOCUMENTS

CANON 1817. Documentum privatum, sive agnitum a parte sive recognitum a iudice, probat adversus auctorem vel subscriptorem et causam ab eis habentes, perinde ac confessio extra iudicium facta; sed per se non habet vim probandi adversus extraneos.

Before the Code an authenticated private writing was, in effect, considered equal to a public document.[54] Since the promulgation of the Code, however, it must be said that an authenticated private instrument in its juridical value can be equal to a public document only in so far as its marks of authentication furnish moral certainty that the instrument was not forged but is genuine. For the authentications made by a public official, or by any other means recognized by law or custom, are indeed public and therefore furnish proof of the genuineness of the authorship, but only of that. The authentication does not change the nature of a private instrument.[55]

Since the purpose of the authentication of a private writing is to insure its genuineness, namely, that it is really the writing of the one to whom it is attributed, it is evident that canon 1817

---

[52] *Canonical Evidence in Marriage Cases,* p. 233.

[53] Cf. S.R.R., *Nullitas matrimonii,* 13 iun. 1911, *coram R.P.D. Francisco Heiner, dec.* XXIV—*Decisiones,* III (1911), 262-263.

[54] Reiffenstuel, *Ius Canonicum Universum,* lib. II, tit. 22, n. 7.

[55] Roberti, *De Processibus,* II, n. 371, p. 101, note 1.

has reference to these writings.[56] If the genuineness is not assured by the acknowledged modes of authentication before the trial, then this assurance must be obtained when the document is produced in court, either through the acknowledgment of the author himself or through the recognition of the judge.[57] For private documents have no probative value or efficacy unless they are produced in court and are there either acknowledged by the party to whom they are attributed and against whom they are presented or, if he denies authorship, are recognized and declared genuine by the sentence of the judge.[58] The one and only distinction that the Code makes in relation to private documents, as far as their probative value is concerned, consists in the differentiation between those which have and those which have not been accorded recognition in the court.[59] In the case of authenticated private writings the judge merely acknowledges the marks of authentication, for the genuineness was proved before the trial. The easiest and by the same token the most satisfactory means of obtaining this recognition of genuineness for non-authenticated instruments is to receive the acknowledgment of the writer, made by word or by writing in the presence of the judge. But it is not required as a condition that this acknowledgment be made by the author of the document expressly. For when a private document is produced in court against a litigant and he has been notified of its existence and of the intention of his opponent to use it against him, then the judge may declare the document to be genuine if no denial has been made of its genuineness within

---

[56] "Documento auténtico. Es el que hace fe por si mismo sin ningúm otro adminículo, . . . como la hace todo documento privado después de reconocido;"—Muniz, *Procedimientos Eclesiásticos,* III, n. 361; "Documentis privatis recognitis a iudice videntur aequiparanda documenta aliis etiam modis authentizata, e.g., ex appositione sigilli magistratus etc."—Coronata, *Institutiones,* n. 1348, note 7.

[57] "Documenta *recognita a iudice* sunt documenta quae iudicis sententia sive definitiva sive incidentali genuina declarata sunt."—Coronata, *Institutiones,* n. 1348.

[58] Canons 1817 and 1819.

[59] ". . . hoy los documentos privados se clasifican en reconocidos y no reconocidos, . . . y no hay otra destinción en el Código.—Muniz, *Procedimientos Eclesiásticos,* III, n. 371, note 1. Cf. Coronata, *loc. cit.*

the time granted for this by the judge or within the duration of the probatory period of the trial when no time-limit for such denial has been set by the court.[60] It rather frequently happens that the litigant denies the authorship of the writing. In this case the party who produced the document must prove its genuineness, to the satisfaction of the judge, by the ordinary means, e.g., by the testimony of witnesses, by the comparison which is made between this and other documents which are known or acknowledged by their author as being genuine, etc.

A. Legal Efficacy Against Third Parties

As has been seen, a public document exerts its full probative force against all, even against those who were not parties to the contract, fact or transaction. But private documents do not have this value of proof, even though they have been acknowledged as genuine by the author or have been recognized as such by the judge. This acknowledgment or recognition connotes nothing more than a method and means employed in connection with or during the process of a trial for the authentication of a document which was not authenticated before. The wording of the canon clearly denies of private documents what it asserts of public instruments, namely, that the latter establish proof also against outsiders. But, it is also true that even public documents fall under the principle, *"res inter alios acta aliis non prodesse nec nocere posse."* Consequently, both public and private instruments have this characteristic in common, that only the parties to the contract are bound to the substance of the agreement. In the public document the notary furnishes full credibility concerning the individual acts of the recorded agreement or transaction, but in a private instrument the agreement is *inter privatos* and the authentication of the notary furnishes credibility only regarding the genuineness of the signatures. He can not give any assurances of the truth of the facts as recorded, because the document was not drawn up by him nor in his presence when the agreement

---

[60] The probatory period officially opens immediately after the *litis contestatio* (canon 1731, 2°) and continues up to the close of the trial (*conclusio in causa*). Cf. canon 1860, § 1; Roberti, *De Processibus*, II, n. 227, p. 30.

was made.[61] It logically follows, therefore, that those who are not parties to the contract are not bound to place any credibility in the truth of the contents of a private document, even though it has been acknowledged or judicially proved to be genuine.[62] It can not, therefore, of itself be of any judicial value against outsiders.

The canon adds the phrase *"per se,"* because if outsiders or third parties acknowledge the true facts of the document, or if a notary not only attested to the genuineness of the authorship but also to the truth of its contents, or if there are other corroborative proofs, it proves against outsiders in like manner as a confession made out of court. Furthermore, a private instrument in relation to outsiders is to be considered as a private testimony and must be evaluated according to the norms given for the evaluation of depositions made by private witnesses.[63]

B. Legal Efficacy Against the Author of the Document

Even though the private instrument is acknowledged as genuine by the author himself, or is established as genuine despite his denial, the document does not thereby necessarily furnish all the elements of proof against its author. For the canon expressly states that private instruments which have been acknowledged by a party as his own, or which have been recognized as genuine by the judge, furnish proof in the same measure as an extrajudicial confession against the author or signatory, and also against those who derive their claim to some right or property through the author or signatory of such documents.[64] Thus the rule of canon 1817 is certainly not in agreement with the doctrine of some of the older authors who asserted that such an acknowledgment, even

---

[61] Lega-Bartoccetti, *Commentarius,* II, 798.

[62] To the contrary Smith, *Elements of Ecclesiastical Law,* II, *Ecclesiastical Trials* (New York, 1882), n. 868:—"The former [authentic private instruments] prove either for or against their writers or a third party." Likewise Reiffenstuel, *Ius Canonicum Universum,* lib. II, tit. 22, nn. 12, 174.

[63] Cappello, *Summa Iuris Canonici,* III, n. 281.

[64] Canon 1817; Muniz, *Procedimientos Eclesiásticos,* III, n. 378:—". . . el reconocimiento de un documento privado no es confesión judicial de su contenido."

though it was extrajudicial, nevertheless had the force of a judicial confession.[65]

The law of Gregory XVI for the Papal States[66] attributed full value of proof to signed private documents against the one who was the alleged signatory. Lega applied the same principle to Canon Law. He argued that the one who brings forth a signed instrument implicitly produces a confession concerning the truths of the facts described therein, if the facts pertain to the controverted question. Furthermore, so Lega contended, if anyone does not repudiate a written instrument which is signed by him and produced against him by the adversary, namely, by showing that the document is not genuine, then such a one thereby admits that he signed the document and, by way of consequence, plainly admits that the document contains the implications charged against him by the adversary.[67] However, the Code places the burden of proof on the one who produces a private document. If the genuineness of the document is not already evident from its authentication, it

[65] Smith, *Ecclesiastical Trials*, n. 868; Reiffenstuel, *Ius Canonicum Universum*, lib. II, tit. 22, nn. 170, 173; Schmalzgrueber, *Ius Ecclesiasticum Universum*, lib. III, tit. 22, n. 77.

[66] *Regolamento legislativo e giudiziario*, n. 615. This *Regolamento* is found among the *Acta Gregorii Papae* (4 vols., Romae, 1901-1904), in volume IV, on pages 300-410. Although it was promulgated in 1834 for the use of all secular tribunals in the Papal States, and consequently was not enacted as ecclesiastical legislation nor was ever acknowledged to be binding in ecclesiastical tribunals, yet it exerted considerable influence even in the field of Canon Law. Cf. Lega, *De Iudiciis Ecclesiasticis Civilibus*, I, *Prooemium*, p. 17, note 2.

[67] "Instrumenta privata *subscripta* fidem faciunt in foro eccles. iuxta principium enunciatum in art. 615 *cod. Greg. cit.*, nempe: *'Scripturae privatae plenam probationem faciunt in iudicio adversus eos qui illas subscripserunt, donec subscriptio legali modo non fuerit reprobata . . .'* Ille enim qui producit instrumentum a se subscriptum implicitam edit *confessionem* de veritate factorum ibi descriptorum, quae pertinent ad rem controversam.—Praeterea qui instrumentum a se subscriptum et ab adversario productum non reprobat, demonstrans hoc non esse genuinum, iam fatetur instrumentum a se fuisse subscriptum, et hinc apertam continere confessionem intentionis adversarii."—Lega, *De Iudiciis Ecclesiasticis Civilibus*, I, n. 513. Cf. also Roberti, *De Processibus*, II, n. 371, note 1, and De Luca, *Theatrum Veritatis et Iustitiae* (16 vols., Coloniae Agrippinae, 1706), XV, *De Iudiciis*, disc. 29, n. 20. Hereafter cited simply as *De Iudiciis*.

must be proved either through the acknowledgment of the alleged author or by means of a judicial recognition, as was seen above. Otherwise the private document can not be used for adverse proof. This is clearly implied in the very wording of canon 1817.

It is to be noted that the acknowledgment pertains merely to the authorship, and not to the truth of the facts related in the document. While the author admits indeed that he wrote the document or signed his name to it, he may nevertheless rightfully contend that it does not pertain to the case at issue, that he was unaware of its exact contents when he signed it, that he affixed his signature under the stress of duress, undue influence, etc.[68]

It may appear that such defenses are of an affirmative nature, which must be pleaded, and that the burden of proof is upon the party alleging such defenses.[69] However, a civil court of appeals of the State of New York[70] ruled in such cases that, when a party sues upon a contract, he must sustain the burden of proving a contract valid in its inception. In the case referred to by the court, the plaintiff sued upon a written agreement to compromise and settle a suit. The answer denied the material allegations of the complaint and alleged illegality of agreement, conspiracy, fraud and duress. In the language of the court:[71] "The defenses of conspiracy and duress were in reality and in substance negative, in effect alleging that there was no legal contract, and that it never had a valid inception. These defenses pertain to the fact which took place at the time the contract was alleged to have been executed and became the *res gesta,* upon which the validity of the contract depends. This class of defenses is distinguishable from those affirmative defenses which are based upon facts occurring subsequently to the execution of a contract, in which it may be changed, altered, modified or settled. It, therefore, follows that the plaintiff, in undertaking to prove the contract upon which his action is based, had cast upon him the burden of establishing, by a preponderance of evidence, that it was a good and valid contract

---

[68] Cf. Roberti, *De Processibus,* II, n. 371, p. 101.

[69] "Onus probandi incumbit ei qui asserit."—Canon 1748, § 1.

[70] Murray v. Norwood, 192 N. Y. 172, 84 N. E. 958. The civil law is to be followed in matters pertaining to contracts. Cf. canon 1529.

[71] *Ibidem,* p. 77.

having a legal inception which was binding upon the defendant, and that burden of proof continued with him throughout the case."[72]

The affirmative defenses based on facts subsequent to the execution of the contract in which it may be changed, altered, modified or settled would amount to a qualified or complex confession and must be considered and judged accordingly.[73]

It is evident, however, that if not only the genuineness of the signature but also the truth of the recorded facts is admitted, then such an acknowledgment in court is nothing less than a judicial confession. If the document pertains to private affairs and if the admission entails an adverse implication for the author of the document or for the signatory, then such a confession begets full proof in favor of the opponent.[74]

Ordinarily further proof seems superfluous if a fact is admitted by an adversary, but the Code admits judicial confession as complete proof only in private affairs. In cases wherein the public welfare is concerned, e.g., the cases which deal with the validity of marriage, the validity of sacred orders, the punishment of criminals, etc., judicial confession does not relieve the opponent from the necessity of further proving the case.[75]

---

[72] For other cases similar to the Murray v. Norwood case cf. Farmer's Loan and Trust Co. v. Siefke, 144 N. Y. 354, 39 N. E. 358; Cohen v. Gurman (1941), Supreme Court, N. Y. 28 N. Y. S 2nd. 917. In cases prior to the Murray v. Norwood case the New York courts held that such defenses were affirmative and consequently the burden of proof was upon the party alleging them. Cf. Speling v. Ball, 10 App. Div. 290, 41 N. Y. S. 889; Swift v. Poole, 172 App. Div. 10, 157 N. Y. S. 928; Doheny v. Lacy, 168 N. Y. 213, 61 N. E. 255; Green v. Roworth, 113 N. Y. 462, 21 N. E. 165.

[73] Cf. *infra*, p.

[74] Canon 1751. In one place Reiffenstuel, in referring to the maxim, "*Propria confessio est optima probati,*" calls the judicial confession fullest proof.—*Ius Canonicum Universum,* lib. II, tit. 22, n. 12. Cf. also S.R.R., *Nullitas matrimonii,* 15 novembris, 1909, *coram R.P.D. Gustavo Persiani,* dec. XVI, n. 7—*Decisiones,* I (1909), 139; c. 2, X, *de cohabitatione clericorum et mulierum,* III, 2. In another place Reiffenstuel states that properly considered the confession is rather a revelation of the proof:—"Unde consequens est, quod confessio proprie non sit probatio, sed potius revelatio probationis."—*Ibidem,* n. 14.

[75] Canon 1715.

If private documents have been authenticated before the trial, or if they have been duly acknowledged or judicially recognized during the process of the trial, they have the same probative value against the author or signatory as an extrajudicial confession.[76] In order therefore to understand what is the probative force of private documents the judicial import of an extrajudicial confession must be considered.

1—Extrajudicial Confession

The Code defines an extrajudicial confession as a written or oral confession or admission made to one's opponent or to others outside the court.[77] Regarding its probative value, canon 1753 states that, if this confession is introduced in court, it is left to the discretion of the judge, after considering all the attendant circumstances, to determine its weight. The value, therefore, of an extrajudicial confession and by the same token that of an authenticated private document is not defined by the Code, but is left for its determination to the prudent discretion of the judge, which is reached by his careful weighing of all the circumstances that may affect its appraisal, e.g., the quality of the person, the circumstance under which it was made, etc.

With the view to aiding the judge in fulfilling this broad yet important duty imposed upon him by the Code, it will be found useful to consider the teaching of the pre-Code jurists and writers relative to the subject.

A general rule regarding the juridical value of an extrajudicial confession is found in both the Roman and the Decretal Law. This rule holds that an extrajudicial confession made before an adversary, if it relate to the case and bears upon contentious matters, is considered sufficient evidence to relieve the said ad-

[76] ". . . licet documentum privatum dicatur habere vim confessionis extraiudicialis, maioris tamen efficaciae esse quam ipsam extraiudicialem confessionem, tum quia scriptura semper loquitur et ideo censetur loqui etiam in praesentia iudicis, tum quia cum maiori deliberatione et cautela solemus aliquid scribere quam loqui."—Coronata, *Institutiones,* n. 1348, p. 253, note 5.

[77] Canon 1753.

versary from the burden of further proof.[78] And the judge, all other things being equal, may pass sentence against the one making such a confession. The reason is found in the presumption that a person would not, in the presence of his adversary or of the one representing him, acknowledge a fictitious obligation and thereby recognize to be present a cause out of which a special duty or indebtedness will be charged against him.[79] But, on the other hand, it can readily be understood how anyone would not be so cautious in making an assertion before another whom he believes either not to be able or not to be desirous to use such an assertion against him. For this reason an extrajudicial assertion which was made not in the presence of an adversary would be considered as having the value of part (*semi-plena*) proof and, therefore, necessarily requires corroborative evidence if it is to prove, for instance, that the confession was made seriously, i.e., not motivated by anger, fear or undue persuasion, and that it was made with conviction and with a certain knowledge of the obligation.[80] It is to be especially noted that, no matter in what manner an extrajudicial confession is produced in court, whether by means of the testimony of witnesses or by the means of writing, the judge must assure himself that the confession was made in connection with the case at issue.[81]

As previously stated, the foregoing applies only to civil or contentious cases. In criminal cases an extrajudicial confession of any crime does not beget full or complete proof. For, as Santi asserts, in proving one guilty of any crime unquestionable proof is

---

[78] D. (22, 3) 25, 4; c. 10, X, *de probationibus*, II, 19; c. 14, X, *de fide instrumentorum*, II, 22, cum Glossa ad v. *Sed si causa*. Cf. also Glossa in can. c. 15, C. III, q. 9.

[79] ". . . presente adversario, non praesumitur quis velle fictitiam obligationem palam facere, simulque causam exprimere per quam debitum speciale cognoscitur."—Santi, *Praelectiones Juris Canonici* (2 vols., Ratisbonae, 1886), lib. II, tit. 18, n. 5.

[80] Santi, *loc. cit.*

[81] "Quare defectus mentionis causae aliquando imminuit vim probativam confessionis, nec proinde eximit adversarium ab onere probandi."—*Loc. cit.* Cf. c. 14, X, *de fide instrumentorum*, II, 22, cum glossa ad v. *Sed si causa.*

necessary not only regarding the identity of the person accused of the crime but also the moral imputability of the act.[82]

In enumerating some of the circumstances which may aid the judge in deciding whether an extrajudicial confession, which was made not in the presence of the adversary, but nevertheless seriously, that is, with conviction and with a certain knowledge of the obligation, Santi mentions the fact of its having been made in writing, especially by means of a written instrument.[83] Santi evidently wishes to distinguish, on the one hand, between personal letters or notes and, on the other, writings drawn up with the expressed purpose of proving a fact at some future time. And with reason does he make such a distinction. For in personal communication, although it be made in writing, there is a sense of security that the contents of such a writing will enjoy immunity from publicity or will be kept in strict confidence. In the latter case, however, the author or signatory can expect the contents of the instrument to be made public and to be used against him in court if circumstances arise which justify his opponent in doing so.

Nevertheless, even if the confession was made by means of a

---

[82] ". . . ad demonstrandum aliquem reum fuisse criminis alicujus . . . requiruntur probationes, omni exceptione majores quae nempe in animo judicis certam inducant persuasionem non solum de auctore delicti, sed etiam de moralitate actionis, et de gradu culpabilitatis."—*Ibidem,* n. 6; "Confessio extraiudicialis in causis criminalibus plenam vim probandi non habet, ideoque sola non sufficit ad pronuntiandam condemnationem."—Wernz-Vidal, *Ius Canonicum,* VI, n. 455; "In this case (criminal trial) an extrajudicial confession is no proof whatever, not even semi-proof. The conviction of a criminal must be, as the canons say, by evidence clearer than sunshine (probationibus luce meridiana clarioribus). Such a confession, when properly brought before, and proved to, the court will make at most presumptive evidence, or furnish grounds for special inquiry."—Droste, *Canonical Procedure in Disciplinary and Criminal Cases of Clerics* (edited by the Rev. Sebastian G. Messmer, 1887, New York: Benziger Brothers), p. 99.

[83] "Quod si vero absente parte adversa edatur confessio extrajudicialis cum causa, ea vim habet probationis semi-plenae, scilicet per se non relevat alium collitigantem ab omni onere probationis, nisi alia adminicula concurrant, quae ostendant confessionem fuisse serio, et ex animo persuasione, et ex certa scientia obligationis. Ita ex. gr. si confessio absente adversa parte emissa fuerit per scripturam, vel eo magis per instrumentum."—*Ibidem,* n. 5.

judicial instrument, this fact does not necessarily exclude all possibility of danger that the instrument was procured through deceit, force or fear. The judge should be cognizant of that fact, especially if the defendant alleges such charges. Thus, in practice, no matter in what form an extrajudicial confession is introduced in court, the principle enunciated in canon 1753 will apply. It will be left to the prudent discretion of the judge, after he has considered all the attendant circumstances, to determine what weight attaches by way of probative value to the extant extrajudicial confession.

2—Partitioned Confession

Relative to the subject of private documents there arises the question concerning the partitioned or split confession. This matter is treated at length by Lega-Bartoccetti.[84] Their discussion concerns explicitly not only confessions made in court, but also those made extra-judicially. And when this extrajudicial confession is made in writing it is a private document. Consequently what is said by them regarding a qualified confession is equally applicable to private documents which contain such a qualified or complex confession. The question raised by the above quoted authors is whether or not a qualified or complex confession can be divided, or, in other words, whether or not the judge or plaintiff may accept only that part of the confession which favors the plaintiff and reject that part which favors him who made the confession.

As explained by Lega-Bartoccetti,[85] a confession is not simple but qualified if there is added to the confession some restrictive qualification, as for instance: "I promised you one hundred dollars but on the condition that you would do this or that"; or "You gave me one hundred dollars which you owed me by reason of something you borrowed." A non-qualified but complex confession is had if two distinct facts are asserted, of which one does not of its nature qualify or restrict the other, as for example: "I owed

[84] *Commentarius,* II, 650-655.

[85] *Commentarius,* II, p. 650. Cf. Reiffenstuel, *Ius Canonicum Universum,* lib. II, tit. 18, n. 14.

you one hundred dollars but I have already paid the debt"; or "I owe you one hundred dollars for materials borrowed from you but you owe me the same amount for some other reason." As is evident, these examples refer to civil or contentious cases. An example of a qualified confession in a criminal case would be the following: "I wounded a man but it was in self-defence"; or "I said injurious things about a certain individual but as a joke."

Now, as to the question proposed above, it should be stated that the canons of the Code are silent about the matter. Furthermore, the question has never been solved by any authentic legal document in the pre-Code law. Wherefore, the teaching of approved canonists and the jurisprudence of canonical procedure must be followed.[86]

Reiffenstuel holds that a qualified confession may not be divided in such a manner that only the part which harms the cause of the one making the confession is accepted. For, as he asserts, a qualified confession should be considered as an undivided whole which is either entirely accepted or completely rejected.[87] This rule may be applied, however, only when there is no presumption of law standing against the added qualification. For a legal presumption in the absence of contrary evidence is considered in law as the equivalent of complete proof. Consequently, under its weight the qualified part of the confession must be regarded as refuted and therefore rejected.[88] Furthermore, this rule does not apply when, by direct proof, it is established that the truth is to be found in the pure confession and not in the qualifying portion thereof.[89] It is not necessary that these presumptions or proofs be expressly produced after the qualified confession has been

---

[86] *Loc. cit.* Many of the modern civil Codes nave determined the question. Thus the French (Art. 1360), Italian (Art. 1356) and Spanish (Art. 1233) civil Codes do not allow confessions to be split, but the civil Code of Holland (Art. 1961) leaves the matter to the prudent discretion of the judge.

[87] "Confessio qualificata debet vel tota recipi vel tota respui."—*Ius Canonicum Universum,* lib. II, tit. 18, n. 120; "Nemo non videt incivile esse scindere talem confessionem."—Coronata, *Institutiones,* n. 1348, p. 253, note 2.

[88] Reiffenstuel, *loc. cit.;* Schmalzgrueber, *Ius Ecclesiasticum Universum,* lib. II, tit. 18, n. 34; Lega-Bartoccetti, *Commentarius,* II, 651.

[89] Reiffenstuel, *Ius Canonicum Universum,* lib. II, tit. 18, n. 120.

made. They may be inferred from what has already been proffered by the plaintiff.[90]

Cardinal De Luca (1614-1683) offered a practical conclusion in this question. He taught that the whole matter, in civil cases, had to be considered as referring to fact rather than to right. It would, as he stated, be incorrect to consider only generalities, because, in fact, the circumstances of individual cases, according to the prudent and well tempered decision of the judge, should decide the matter, especially as to whether or not there is present in the qualifying part of the confession any foundation for truth.[91] Hence the Cardinal, while he did not deny the rule that a qualified confession should not, in principle, be divided, yet asserted that it frequently suffered exceptions in the estimation of the judge who, from the acts and proofs as well as from the presumptions flowing from them, repudiated the qualifying portion, and considered the qualified confession to be true as to its simple assertion. Thus it may be concluded with Lega-Bartoccetti[92] that in practice it is dangerous to enunciate a rule which the judge very often is unable to follow. For although the plaintiff does not have the right to divide or split the confession in such a manner that it favors his purpose, nevertheless, the judge may do so if he is certain from the acts and proofs that the added qualification has no foundation in truth. This conclusion is likewise sanctioned by the practice of the Sacred Roman Rota.[93]

---

[90] Lega-Bartoccetti, *Commentarius,* II, 652.

[91] *De Iudiciis,* disc. 23, n. 33: "Et in summa, universa ista materia confessionis in civilibus, facti potius quam iuris censenda est, erronee ex solis generalitatibus regulanda, cum revera ex prudenti ac recto beneque regulato iudicis arbitrio singulorum casuum circumstantiae rem decidere debeant, potissimum vero an verisimilitudinis vel inverisimilitudinis fomentum accedat."

[92] *Commentarius,* II, 653.

[93] S.R.R., *Decisiones Recentiores, coram R.P.D., Lugdunen,* 10 dec., 1608, decis. 167, n. 17, pars 1; *coram R.P.D. Buratto,* 22 maii, 1615, decis. 699, n. 2, pars II; *coram R.P.D. Manzanedo,* 28 nov., 1612, decis. 452, n. 9, et decis. 758, n. 4, pars III; *coram R.P.D. Talia,* 17 aprilis, 1673, decis. 80, n. 9, pars XVIII, tom. I; *coram R.P.D. Merlino,* 3 dec., 1627, decis. 118, n. 26, pars V, tom. I; *coram R.P.D. Meltio,* 24 nov., 1655, decis. 91, n. 17, pars XII; *coram R.P.D. Dunozetto,* 9 dec., 1619, decis. 154, n. 17; *coram R.P.D. Ubaldo,* 20 martii, 1620, decis. 195, n. 15, pars IV, tom. 2.

As asserted above, this conclusion has been considered in the light of civil cases. In criminal cases authors seem to agree that a qualified confession can be and as a rule is divided.[94] For when one confesses an injury which he has inflicted but qualifies his confession with excuses, e.g., "I killed, wounded or mutilated a man, but did so in self-defense," the qualifying part is not to be believed or accepted unless it is proved. Against such a one, the authors assert, there always stands the presumption of law by virtue of which he who *de facto* has injured another is presumed to have done so intentionally and with malice.[95]

Regarding the complex confession, since in making such a confession two distinct facts are asserted, one of which does not of its nature qualify the other, it is evident that it should be split and each portion thereof considered separately.

From the above considerations it must be concluded that the principle of a purely legal appraisal in the matter of private documents is not sanctioned by the Code of Canon Law. For the Code admits all private writings as proof only if and when they are produced in court and appear to the judge to be plainly of value. Thus, depending upon its individual nature, a private document may furnish complete proof, partial proof, or be destitute of all probative value, against its author or signatory, according to the discretion of the judge when the latter has considered all the

---

[94] Lega-Bartoccetti, *Commentarius*, II, p. 653, note 2: "In hac materia (de iudiciis criminalibus) autem vidimus omnes DD. opinari confessionem qualificatam posse scindi."

[95] "Si reus confiteatur se occidisse, sed ad defensionem propriam, vel si dicat se contumeliosa verba sparsisse aliquem, sed non animo injuriandi; si qualitatem annexam non probet, non creditur, sed statur confessione deposita quoad substantiam, rejecta qualitate, eo quod contra hanc militet praesumptio juris, quae est, ut quilibet occidens, vel dicens verba contumeliosa censeatur habere animum offendendi, quare, ut elidatur haec praesumptio, probatione est opus; alias ita confessus damnabitur a judice, non tamen ad paenam ordinarium, e.g., capitis pro homicidio sic confesso, sed aliam meliorem."—Schmalzgrueber, *Ius Ecclesiasticum Universum*, lib. II, tit. 18, n. 33. Lega-Bartoccetti (*Commentarius*, II, 654) see no reason for making a distinction between civil and criminal cases, for both result in the same conclusion, namely, when there is a presumption militating against the qualifying portion of the confession it is held to be judicially refuted, and the pure or simple confession remains.

circumstances attending the case. The judge will, therefore, be on his guard to avoid two extremes. He must not attribute to private documents more value than is inherent therein; but, on the other hand, he must not underestimate their worth. To avoid these two extremes the greatest precaution will be necessary, in each individual case, when the judge examines the document. He will use all the means available to arrive at a well-founded and prudent decision.

Although it has been stated above that strictly private or personal writings do not, by their very nature, furnish the same probative value as a written instrument which is drawn up with the expressed purpose of proving a fact or transaction at some future time, nevertheless, the 1936 Instruction of the Sacred Congregation of the Sacraments reveals the important rôle that even these writings can play, especially in establishing the status of a marriage if its validity has been impugned.[96]

After asserting the fact that letters which the parties wrote to each other, or to other persons before or after the marriage (*sed tempore non suspecto*), can be private documents of no little weight or importance, especially in cases of fear and conditional consent, provided that their genuineness[97] and the time[98] of their writing are beyond question, the Instruction advises the auditor not to delay in obtaining these letters by warning the parties and the witnesses that they must present to the tribunal all such letters which may be in their possession.[99] Due to the fact that personal letters are of a strictly private and confidential nature, there is more likelihood that they will reflect the intention and sentiments of the parties at a definite period of time.

---

[96] S. C. de Sacr., *Instructio servanda a tribunalibus dioecesanis in pertractandis causis de nullitate matrimoniorum,* 15 aug. 1936, art. 162-169—*AAS,* XXVIII (1936), 313-361, especially p. 345.

[97] The Instruction (Art. 163, n. 1) uses the term "authenticity." But it is evident that it refers to and means the genuineness of the authorship of the writings.

[98] The time at which these letters were written is a very important consideration. Very often it constitutes the determining factor in evaluating these writings. Cf. *ibidem,* Art. 164. For a very fine illustration cf. Doheny, *Canonical Procedure in Matrimonial Cases,* p. 284.

[99] *Ibidem,* Art. 163, nn. 1, 2.

The use and importance of such letters as well as of other private annotations are likewise revealed in the decisions of the Sacred Roman Rota. For in reading some of its decisions one can not but note that without such means of evidence the true facts of the case would have been very difficult if not impossible to prove.[100]

---

[100] E.g., cf. S.R.R., *Nullitas matrimonii,* 29 dec., 1911, *coram R.P.D. Francisco Heiner,* dec. XLV, n. 13:—"Etenim epistolae ab auctore scriptae, ex quibus directius quinam fuerit ipsius animus eruitur, certo certius plene probant. . . . Etsi enim agatur de scripturis privatis, tamen sunt optimum medium probandi illud quod est in votis actoris."—*Decisiones,* III (1911), 524. For other examples cf. S.R.R., *Nullitas matrimonii,* 10 febr. 1926, *coram R.P.D. Andrea Jullien,* dec. V, n. 7—*Decisiones,* XVIII (1926), 27; *S.R.R., Nullitas matrimonii,* 24 febr. 1926, *coram R.P.D., Andrea Jullien,* dec. VIII, n. 19—*Decisiones,* XVIII (1926), 57; S.R.R., *Nullitas matrimonii,* 4 aug. 1922, *coram R.P.D. Raphaele Chimenti,* dec. XXVII—*Decisiones,* XIV (1922), 253 sq; S.R.R., *Nullitas matrimonii,* 13 febr. 1925, *coram R.P.D. Francisco Solieri,* dec. X, n. 6—*Decisiones,* XVII (1925), 77. For examples establishing the fact that there was no duress or other hindrance or impediment cf. S.R.R., *Nullitas matrimonii,* 6 iul. 1914, *coram R.P.D. Ioanne Prior,* dec. XXI—*Decisiones,* XV (1914), 275; S.R.R., *Nullitas matrimonii,* 9 mart. 1915, *coram R.P.D. Seraphino Many,* dec. VIII—*Decisiones,* VII (1915), 88; S.R.R., *Nullitas matrimonii,* 17 aug. 1916, *coram Friderico Cattani Amadori,* dec. XXVII—*Decisiones,* VIII (1916), 300; S.R.R., *Nullitas matrimonii,* 11 iun. 1920, *coram R.P.D. Petro Rossetti,* dec. XV—*Decisiones,* XII (1920), 135; S.R.R., *Nullitas matrimonii,* 1 iul. 1920, *coram R.P.D. Ioanne Prior,* dec. XIX—*Decisiones,* XII (1920), 185. The Rota even sustained the assertion of the plaintiff against that of the respondent and against the entry made in the parochial marriage record, regarding the domicile of the spouse at the time of the marriage, on the strength of bakery bills, checks drawn for the payment of furniture and a lease of property dated from the time just previous to the marriage, in which writings the party's place of domicile was noted as the plaintiff had stated.—S.R.R., *Nullitas matrimonii,* 4 mart. 1916, *coram R.P.D. Iosepho Mori,* dec. VI—*Decisiones,* VIII (1916), 71. Cf. also S.R.R., *Nullitas matrimonii,* 21 ian. 1911, *coram R.P.D. Seraphino Many,* dec. III—*Decisiones,* III (1911), 23; S.R.R., *Nullitas matrimonii,* 24 mart. 1911, *coram R.P.D., Seraphino Many,* dec. XV—*Decisiones,* III (1911), 158; S.R.R., *Nullitas matrimonii,* 9 febr. 1920, *coram R.P.D. Friderico Cattani Amadori,* dec. V—*Decisiones,* XII (1920), 39.

ARTICLE IV. DEFECTIVE DOCUMENTS

CANON 1818. Si abrasa, correcta, interpolata aliove vitio documenta infecta demonstrentur, iudicis est aestimare an et quanti huiusmodi documenta facienda sint.

The present canon is applicable to both public and private documents. Thus an erasure, interpolation, correction or any other defect appearing in either a public or a private instrument may or may not affect its probative value. It is the right and duty of the judge, after carefully examining the document and making use of all the necessary means to arrive at a prudent decision, to determine if and to what degree credibility must be accorded to the defective document.

A public document, then, may reveal erasures, interpolations or corrections; or it may have other defects, and still retain its original full probative force. An illustrating example of this fact is found in a decision of the Sacred Roman Rota under the date of December 6, 1909. The case was one in which a priest had falsely dated a marriage record in order to make two children, which were born in consequence of illicit relations on the part of the couple before the marriage, appear as legitimate. In the trial regarding the nullity of the marriage it was contended that, since the date was proved fasle, the entire content of the document was to be considered false and useless as evidence. But the Rota decided otherwise. Its contention was that there had been a motive for falsifying the date. To suppose in addition that the priest had drawn up a document without performing the marriage was absurd.[101]

On the other hand, the date can become the determining factor without which the document would be entirely useless. An obvious example is that in which the validity of a marriage is impugned in view of the existence of a bond of marriage at the time when the later marriage was contracted. If, in this case, it is claimed that the first marriage was rightfully dissolved be-

[101] S.R.R., *Nullitas matrimonii,* 6 dec. 1909, *coram R.P.D. Gustavo Persiani,* dec. XVIII—*Decisiones,* I (1909), 155-163, especially p. 158.

fore the second marriage was contracted, it will be necessary that the death certificate of the first spouse, or the sentence of nullity of, or dispensation from, the first marriage, together with the certificate of the second marriage, be exhibited and a diligent comparison be made especially regarding the dates set forth in the respective documents.[102]

For a reason similar to that which supported the decision of Innocent III, in 1203, in a case wherein the documentary witnesses denied having signed their names or taken the part ascribed to them in the written instrument,[103] the Sacred Roman Rota pronounced a marriage invalid for want of consent. In the latter case the priest had made seemingly correct entries in the marriage register. But it was proved by the testimony of those whose names appeared on the certificate as witnesses of the ceremony that one of them had not been present at the marriage, and that the other, although present, had not witnessed any sign of consent on the part of the plaintiff.[104]

In cases like the above noted one, however, it should be remarked that the document would be useless as proof either for or against the validity of the marriage, for as long as the fact of some ceremony is known to have taken place, the presumption of law still stands in favor of the validity of the matrimonial bond. Since the document is not necessary either for the validity of the marriage or for the substance of the act, there still remains the burden of proving that two witnesses other than those whose names appear in the record were not present. In fact, it could readily be assumed that the officiating priest, while having the required number of witnesses, erroneously inscribed their names in the register.

The absence of the proper signature on entries made in public registers does not change their nature, but such entries, when once they are made in the public registers, are still regarded as public documents which furnish juridical credibility.[105] Even if

---

[102] Cf. S.C. de Prop. Fide, instr. a. 1883, n. 42—*Fontes,* n. 4901.

[103] C. 33, X, *de probationibus,* II, 19.

[104] S.R.R., *Nullitas matrimonii,* 23 mart. 1914, *coram R.P.D. Guilelmo Sebastianelli,* dec. XII, n. 10—*Decisiones,* VI (1914), 142-151.

[105] Cf. S.R.R., *Nullitas matrimonii,* 10 iun. 1910, *coram R.P.D. Michael Lega,* dec. XXIII, n. 3—*Decisiones,* II (1910), 221.

the records appear on papers detached from their proper books, they may still be considered as parts of the register, and hence do not thereby lose their value as public instruments, provided that they have the proper marks of authenticity.[106]

Again, an erasure, interpolation, correction or any other intrinsic defect found in a public or private document does not destroy the probative value which the instrument has by its nature, unless these defects occur in a notable or substantial part of the said instrument, e.g., regarding the filled in date and place indicative of the time and locality attending the drafting of the instrument, or regarding the name of the one who drafted the instrument. In a similar way any defects which occur in that part of the document which directly bears upon the matter at issue will destroy the probative force of the document only in so far as they render doubtful the juridical import or meaning of the document.[107] Wherefore the warning of Pope Innocent III must be kept in mind by every judge when in virtue of his office he is called on to preside over the important task of examining documents for the purpose of determining their probative value. Judges in ecclesiastical courts must not lightly discard documents in which there are erasures or corrections, if despite such defects the proper and original import and meaning of such written instruments can nevertheless be ascertained and certified.[108]

The practical questions, then, that should be asked in order to achieve an effective determination of the probative value of any document are these: What precisely is the fact to be proved? Does this particular document prove or assist in proving that fact? If the latter question is answered in the affirmative then the document should be admitted as evidence. Its probative force will be evaluated according to its nature and in the measure of its relation to the case at issue.

---

[106] Cf. S.R.R., *Nullitas matrimonii,* 6 dec. 1909, *coram R.P.D. Gustavo Persiani,* dec. XVIII, n. 7—*Decisiones,* I (1909), 198.

[107] Cf. Augustine, *Ecclesiastical Trials,* p. 261. Cf. also *supra,* p.

[108] Cf. c. 9, X, *de crimine falsi,* V, 20. Cf. also c. 3, X, *de fide instrumentorum,* II, 22; c. 7, X, *de religiosis domibus ut episcopo sint subiectae,* III, 36.

CONCLUSIONS

The following conclusions as deriving from the foregoing study are based either on points not previously considered by canonists since the advent of the Code, or on what appears to be the better opinion concerning points on which the canonists are not of one mind.

1—Although the term "authentic" has different meanings in the various connections in which it is used, the Code indicates that in relation to documents this term refers to the external form of the instrument or to the external marks of public recognition of its genuineness.

2—A public document is a writing which relates an act that was executed by, or in the presence of, a public official acting as such. The act must be properly committed to writing by the same official, or at least signed by him when it has been recorded by another.

3—Entries made in public registers by a person other than the legal custodian of these registers, but under his supervision, are public documents. So too are the entries made by the legal custodian relative to facts of which he has but an indirect knowledge. The public persons to whose charge the law entrusts these registers are bound by their office to enter, or to permit the inscription of, only those facts the veracity of which they can attest and in fact do attest by making the entry themselves or by permitting it to be made by another.

4—Public documents are presumed entirely genuine. This means not only that the instrument is presumed to have been executed by him to whom such a writing is attributed, but that the instrument truly and accurately relates the facts as they occurred. It is this latter presumption that constitutes the essential difference between a public document and a private instrument, even when the latter has been acknowledged or judicially recognized as genuine.

5—In principle the Code awards the same probative force to both civil and ecclesiastical public documents. However, this principle can not always be accepted on its face value when there is question of civil public documents.

6—There is no essential difference, relative to the value of proof, between private documents authenticated before the trial and private documents acknowledged or recognized as genuine during the process of the trial. All are governed by the principle of canon 1817.

7—A private document, although its genuineness is established, does not necessarily furnish all the elements of proof against its author. While admitting the authorship of the document the author may contend that the document does not pertain to the case at issue, that he was unaware of its exact contents when he signed it, or that he affixed his signature under the stress of duress, undue influence, etc.

8—If in the discretion of the judge the above defenses should be admitted, and if they pertain to the facts which took place at the time the contract was alleged to have been executed, then they are negative defenses. Thus the burden of proving that the contract was valid from its inception is placed upon the one producing the document.

BIBLIOGRAPHY

Sources

Acta Apostolicae Sedis, Commentarium Officiale, Romae, 1909-

Acta Gregorii Papae, XVI, 4 vols., Romae, 1901-1904.

Acta Sanctae Sedis, 41 vols., Romae, 1865-1908.

Antiquae Collectiones Decretalium cum Antonii Augustini Episcopi Ilerdensis notis, Illerdae, 1576.

Bullarium Romanum, 25 vols., Augustae Taurinorum, 1857-1872.

Canones et Decreta Concilii Tridentini, Romae, 1845.

Codex Iuris Canonici, Pii X Pontificis Maximi iussu digestus, Benedicti Papae XV auctoritate promulgatus, Romae, 1917.

Corpus Iuris Canonici, editio Lipsiensis post Iusti Henningii Boehmeri curas . . . denuo edidit Aemilius Ludovicus Richter, 2 vols., Lipsiae, 1839.

Corpus Iuris Civilis (Krueger-Mommsen-Schoell-Kroll), 3 vols., Berolini, 1928-1929.

Hardouin, J., *Acta Conciliorum et Epistolae Decretales ac constitutiones Summorum Pontificum,* 12 vols., Parisiis, 1715.

History of the Franks by Gregory of Tours, translated with an introduction by O. M. Dalton, Oxford, 1927.

Mansi, J., *Sacrorum Consiliorum Nova et Amplissima Collectio,* 53 vols. in 59, Paris, Arnhem, Leipzig, 1901-1927.

Monumenta Germaniae Historica, Legum Sectio I, Leges Nationum Germanicarum, Tom. I, ed. Karolus Zeumer, Hannoverae et Lipsiae, 1902.

Monumenta Germanicae Historica, Leges, 5 vols., I-IV ed. Pertz; V, ed. Pertz-Waitz-Brunner, Hannoverae, 1835-1889.

Pallottini, Salvator, *Collectio omnium Conclusionum et Resolutionum Congregationis Concilii ab anno 1564 ad annum 1860,* 18 vols., Romae, 1868-1895.

Quinque Compilationes Antiqae, Nec Non Collectio Canonum Lipsiensis, recognovit et adnotatione critica instruxit Aemilius Friedberg, Lipsiae, Ex Officina Bernhardi Tauchnitz, 1882.

S. Romanae Rotae Decisiones seu Sententiae, Romae, 1912-; *Decisiones Recentiores,* 19 parts in 25 vols., Francofurti-Aureliae-Romae, 1623-1703.

The American and English Encyclopaedia of Law, 2. ed., 30 vols., New York: Edward Thompson Company, 1896-1905.

The Civil Law as Translated by S. P. Scott, 17 vols., Cincinnati, Ohio: The Central Trust Company, 1932.

The Visigothic Code (*Forum Judicum*), translated from the original Latin by S. P. Scott, Boston, 1910.

AUTHORS

Abbot, A., *Trial Evidence,* New York, 1813.

Augustine (Bachofen), Charles, *A Commentary on the New Code of Canon Law,* 8 vols., Vol. VII, *Ecclesiastical Trials,* St. Louis: Herder, 1921.

Bassibey, R., *Le Mariage devant les Tribunaux Ecclésiastiques, Procédure Matrimontale Générale,* Paris: Poitiers, 1899.

Bays, A., *Cases and Materials on Business Law,* 4. ed., Chicago: Callaghan and Company, 1939.

Beste, Udalricus, *Introductio in Codicem,* Collegeville, Minn.: St. John's Abbey Press, 1938.

Bethmann-Hollweg, *Der Römische Civil-process,* 5 vols., Bonn, 1864-1870.

Bouscaren, T. L., *The Canon Law Digest,* 2 vols. and Supplement, Milwaukee: Bruce, 1934-1937; *Supp.,* 1941.

Bresslau, H., *Handbuch der Urkendenlehre für Deutschland und Italien,* 2 vols., Leipzig, 1889. The second edition (1912) of this work was not available to the present writer.

Brunner, H., *Deutsche Rechtsgeschichte,* 2 vols., 1906-1928.

Cappello, F. M., *Summa Iuris Canonici,* 3 vols., Romae: Universitas Gregoriana, I-II, 3. ed., 1938-1939; III, 1936.

Cooper, T., *Institutes of Justinian,* 3. ed., New York, 1852.

Coronata, Matthaeus Conte a, *Institutiones Iuris Canonici,* 5 vols., Taurini (Italia): Marietti, 1928-1936.

Costa, Emilio, *Profilo Storico del Processo Civile Romano,* Roma, 1918.

De Angelis, P., *Praelectiones Juris Canonici,* 4 vols., Romae, 1877-1887.

De Luca, Ioannes Baptista, *Theatrum Veritatis et Iustitiae,* 16 vols., Coloniae Agrippinae, 1706.

Devoti, Joannes, *Jus Canonicum Universum et Privatum,* 3 vols., Romae, 1803.

Doheny, W. J., *Canonical Procedure in Matrimonial Cases,* Milwaukee: Bruce, 1938.

Droste, Francis, *Canonical Procedure in Disciplinary and Criminal Cases of Clerics,* ed. by Sebastian G. Messmer, New York, 1897.

Eichmann, E., *Das Prozeszrecht des Codex Iuris Canonici,* Paderborn: Schöningh, 1921.

Esmein, A., *Le Mariage en Droit Canonique,* 2. ed., 2 vols., Paris: Decueil Sirey, 1929-1935.

Ferraris, F. Lucius, *Prompta Bibliotheca, Canonica, Iuridica, Moralis, Theologica, necnon Ascetica, Polemica, Rubricistica, Historica,* 9 vols., Romae, 1885-1899.

Ferretti, F. A., *I piccoli archivi ecclesiastici e le piccole biblioteche, riordinate secondo il codice di diritto can. e i principali sinodi diocesani,* Roma, 1918.

Gasparri, P., *Tractatus Canonicus De Matrimonio,* 2 vols., Romae: Typis Polylottis Vaticanis, 1932.

Gudelimus, P., *Commentariorum de Jure Novissimo Libri sex,* Florentiae, 1839.

Hughes, T., *An Illustrated Treatise on the Law of Evidence,* third impression, Chicago: Callaghan and Company, 1907.

Lega, Michael, *Praelectiones De Iudiciis Ecclesiasticis,* 4 vols., Romae, 1896-1901; Vol. I, 2. ed., Romae, 1905.

———, *Commentarius in Iudicia Ecclesiastica iuxta Codicem Iuris Canonici,* curante Victorio Bartoccetti, 3 vols., Romae: Anonima Libraria Cattolica Italiana, 1938-1941.

Maroto, P., *Institutiones Iuris Canonici ad Normam Novi Codicis,* 2 vols., Matriti, 1919-1921.

Mascardus, I., *Conclusiones Omnium Probationum quae in Utroque Jure Quotidie Versantur,* 3 vols., Venetiis, 1593.

Muniz, T., *Procedimientos Eclesiásticos,* 2. ed., 3 vols., Sevilla, Lib. de Sobrino de Izquierdo, no date [1921].

Noval, Joseph, *Commentarium Codicis Iuris Canonici,* Liber IV, *De Processibus,* Pars I, *De Iudiciis,* Augustae Taurinorum: Marietti, 1920.

O'Rourke, J., *Parish Registers,* The Catholic University of America Canon Law Studies, n. 88, Washington, D. C.: The Catholic University of America, 1934.

Panormitanus, Abbas (Nicolaus de Tudeschis), *Commentaria in quinque Libros Decretalium,* 8 vols., Venetiis, 1588.

Pirhing, Ernricus, *Ius Canonicum in V Libros Decretalium,* 5 vols., Dilingae, 1674-1678.

Reiffenstuel, Anacletus, *Ius Canonicum Universum,* 6 vols., Romae, 1831-1834.

Rice, Patrick W., *Proof of Death in Pre-Nuptial Investigation,* The Catholic University of America Canon Law Studies, n. 123, Washington, D. C.: The Catholic University of America Press, 1940.

Roberti, Franciscus, *De Processibus,* 2 vols., Romae: Apud Aedes Facultatis Iuridicae ad S. Apollinaris, 1926.

Santi, Franciscus, *Praelectiones Juris Canonici,* 2 vols., Ratisbonae, 1886.

Schmalzgrueber, Franciscus, *Ius Ecclesiasticum Universum,* 5 vols. in 12, Romae, 1843-1845.

Schmidt, John R., *The Principles of Authentic Interpretation in Canon 17 of the Code of Canon Law,* The Catholic University of America Canon Law Studies, n. 141, Washington, D. C.: The Catholic University of America Press, 1941.

Smith, S. B., *Elements of Ecclesiastical Law,* II, *Ecclesiastical Trials,* New York, 1882.

Stephanus, M., *Commentarius in Novellas Justiniani Imperatoris,* Florentiae, 1843.

Vermeersch, A.,-Creusen, J., *Epitome Iuris Canonici,* Mechliniae-Romae: H. Dessain, I, 6. ed., 1937; II-III, 5. ed., 1934-1936.

Wanenmacher, Francis, *Canonical Evidence in Marriage Cases,* Philadelphia: Dolphin Press, 1935.

Wernz, F. X.,-Vidal, P., *Ius Canonicum,* VI, *De Processibus,* Romae: Universitas Gregoriana, 1927.

Whalen, Donald, *Value of Testimonial Evidence in Marriage Procedure,* The Catholic University of America Canon Law Studies, n. 99, Washington, D. C.: The Catholic University of America, 1935.

Wigmore, John H., *A Pocket Code of the Rules of Evidence in Trials at Law,* Boston: Little, Brown, and Company, 1910.

Woywod, Stanislaus, *A Practical Commentary on the Code of Canon Law,* 3. ed., 3 vols., New York: Wagner, 1929.

Ziegler, A. K., *Church and State in Visigothic Spain,* Washington, D. C.: The Catholic University of America, 1930.

Articles

Brissaud, J., "Contracts, Feudal Period," *The Continental Legal History Series,* 10 vols., Boston: Little, Brown, and Company, 1912-1927, III (1912), 491-512.

Millar, R., "Method of the Proceedings," *The Continental Legal History Series,* VII (1927), 125-178.

Periodical

Zeitschrift der Savigny-Stiftung für Rechtsgeschichte, Romanistische Abteilung, Weimar, 1880-

ABBREVIATIONS

AAS—Acta Apostolicae Sedis
ASS—Acta Sanctae Sedis
CLHS—Continental Legal History Series
Decisiones—S. Romanae Rotae Decisiones seu Sententiae
Fontes—Codicis Iuris Canonici Fontes
MGH—Monumenta Germaniae Historica
S.C.C.—Sacra Congregatio Concilii
S.C. de Prop. Fide—Sacra Congregatio de Propaganda Fide
S.C. de Sacr.—Sacra Congregatio de Disciplina Sacramentorum
S.R.R.—Sacra Romana Rota

BIOGRAPHICAL NOTE

Robert A. Willett was born January 17, 1906, in Springfield, Kentucky, and attended Holy Trinity School in Fredericktown, Kentucky. He received his secondary education in St. Mary's Mission House, Techny, Illinois. His Seminary course was made at St. Meinrad, Indiana. He was ordained to the sacred priesthood on June 10, 1933. After serving as assistant at St. Paul's Church, Owensboro, Kentucky, assistant and later administrator at St. Paul's Church, Louisville, Kentucky, he was enrolled in the School of Canon Law at the Catholic University of America in the fall of 1939 and received the Baccalaureate in Canon Law in June, 1940, the Licentiate in Canon Law in June, 1941.

ALPHABETICAL INDEX

CANON LAW STUDIES

1. Freriks, Rev. Celestine A., C.PP.S., J.C.D., Religious Congregations in Their External Relations, 121 pp., 1916.
2. Galliher, Rev. Daniel M., O.P., J.C.D., Canonical Elections, 117 pp., 1917.
3. Borowski, Rev. Aurelius L., O.F.M., J.C.D., De Confraternitatibus Ecclesiasticis, 136 pp., 1918.
4. Castillo, Rev. Cayo, J.C.D., Disertacion Historico-Canonica sobre la Potestad del Cabildo en Sede Vacante o Impedida del Vicario Capitular, 99 pp., 1919 (1918).
5. Kubelbeck, Rev. William J., S.T.B., J.C.D., The Sacred Penitentiaria and Its Relations to Faculties of Ordinaries and Priests, 129 pp., 1918.
6. Petrovits, Rev. Joseph J.C., S.T.D., J.C.D., The New Church Law On Matrimony, X-461 pp., 1919.
7. Hickey, Rev. John J., S.T.B., J.C.D., Irregularities and Simple Impediments in the New Code of Canon Law, 100 pp., 1920.
8. Klekotka, Rev. Peter J., S.T.B., J.C.D., Diocesan Consultors, 179 pp., 1920.
9. Wanenmacher, Rev. Francis, J.C.D., The Evidence in Ecclesiastical Procedure Affecting the Marriage Bond, 1920 (Printed 1935).
10. Golden, Rev. Henry Francis, J.C.D., Parochial Benefices in the New Code, IV-119 pp., 1921 (Printed 1925).
11. Koudelka, Rev. Charles J., J.C.D., Pastors, Their Rights and Duties According to the New Code of Canon Law, 211 pp., 1921.
12. Melo, Rev. Antonius, O.F.M., J.C.D., De Exemptione Regularium, X-188 pp., 1921.
13. Schaaf, Rev. Valentine Theodore, O.F.M., S.T.B., J.C.D., The Cloister, X-180 pp., 1921.
14. Burke, Rev. Thomas Joseph, S.T.D., J.C.D., Competence in Ecclesiastical Tribunals, IV-117 pp., 1922.
15. Leech, Rev. George Leo, J.C.D., A Comparative Study of the Constitution, "Apostolicae Sedis" and the "Codex Juris Canonici," 179 pp., 1922.
16. Motry, Rev. Hubert Louis, S.T.D., J.C.D., Diocesan Faculties According to the Code of Canon Law, II-167 pp., 1922.
17. Murphy, Rev. George Lawrence, J.C.D., Delinquencies and Penalties in the Administration and Reception of the Sacraments, IV-121 pp., 1923.
18. O'Reilly, Rev. John Anthony, S.T.B., J.C.D., Ecclesiastical Sepulture in the New Code of Canon Law, II-129 pp., 1923.

19. Michalicka, Rev. Wenceslas Cyrill, O.S.B., J.C.D., Judicial Procedure in Dismissal of Clerical Exempt Religious, 107 pp., 1923.
20. Dargin, Rev. Edward Vincent, S.T.B., J.C.D., Reserved Cases According to the Code of Canon Law, IV-103 pp., 124.
21. Godfrey, Rev. John A., S.T.B., J.C.D., The Right of Patronage According to the Code of Canon Law, 153 pp., 1924.
22. Hagedorn, Rev. Francis Edward, J.C.D., General Legislation on Indulgences, II-154 pp., 1924.
23. King, Rev. James Ignatius, J.C.D., The Administration of the Sacraments to Dying Non-Catholics, V-141 pp., 1924.
24. Winslow, Rev. Francis Joseph, A.F.M., J.C.D., Vicars and Prefects Apostolic, IV-149 pp., 1924.
25. Correa, Rev. Jose Servelion, S.T.L., J.C.D., La Potestad Legislativa de la Iglesia Catolica, IV-127 pp., 1925.
26. Dugan, Rev. Henry Francis, A.M., J.C.D., The Judiciary Department of the Diocesan Curia, 87 pp., 1925.
27. Keller, Rev. Charles Frederick, S.T.B., J.C.D., Mass Stipends, 167 pp., 1925.
28. Paschang, Rev. John Linus, J.C.D., The Sacramentals According to the Code of Canon Law, 129 pp., 1925.
29. Pointek, Rev. Cyrillus, O.F.M., S.T.B., J.C.D., De Indulto Exclaustrationis necnon Saecularizationis, XIII-289 pp., 1925.
30. Kearney, Rev. Richard Joseph, S.T.B., J.C.D., Sponsors at Baptism According to the Code of Canon Law, IV-127 pp., 1925.
31. Bartlett, Rev. Chester Joseph, A.M., LL.B., J.C.D., The Tenure of Parochial Property in the United States of America, V-108 pp., 1926.
32. Kilker, Rev. Adrian Jerome, J.C.D., Extreme Unction, V-425 pp., 1926.
33. McCormick, Rev. Robert Emmett, J.C.D., Confessors of Religious, VIII-266 pp., 1926.
34. Miller, Rev. Newton Thomas, J.C.D., Founded Masses According to the Code of Canon Law, VII-93 pp., 1926.
35. Roelker, Rev. Edward G., S.T.D., J.C.D., Principles of Privilege According to the Code of Canon Law, XI-166 pp., 1926.
36. Bakalarczyk, Rev. Richardus, M.I.C., J.U.D., De Novitiatu, VIII-208 pp., 1927.
37. Pizzuti, Rev. Lawrence, O.F.M., J.U.L., De Parochis Religiosis, 1927. (Not printed).
38. Bliley, Rev. Nicholas Martin, O.S.B., J.C.D., Altars According to the Code of Canon Law, XIX-132 pp., 1927.
39. Brown, Mr. Brendan Francis, A.B., LL.M., J.U.D., The Canonical Juristic Personality with Special Reference to Its Status in the United States of America, V-212 pp., 1927.
40. Cavanaugh, Rev. William Thomas, C.P., J.U.D., The Reservation of the Blessed Sacrament, VIII-101 pp., 1927.

41. Doheny, Rev. William J., C.S.C., A.B., J.U.D., Church Property: Modes of Acquisition, X-118 pp., 1927.
42. Feldhaus, Rev. Aloysius H., C.PP.S., J.C.D., Oratories, IX-141 pp., 1927.
43. Kelly, Rev. James Patrick, A.B., J.C.D., The Jurisdiction of the Simple Confessor, X-208 pp., 1927.
44. Neuberger, Rev. Nicholas J., J.C.D., Canon 6 or the Relation of the Codex Juris Canonici to the Preceding Legislation, V-95 pp., 1927.
45. O'Keefe, Rev. Gerald Michael, J.C.D., Matrimonial Dispensations, Powers of Bishops, Priests and Confessors, VIII-232 pp., 1927.
46. Quigley, Rev. Joseph, A.M.. A.B., J.C.B., Condemned Societies, 139 pp., 1927.
47. Zaplotnik, Rev. Johannes Leo, J.C.D., De Vicariis Foraneis, X-142 pp., 1927.
48. Duskie, Rev. John Aloysius, A.B., J.C.D., The Canonical Status of the Orientals in the United States, VIII-196 pp., 1928.
49. Hyland, Rev. Francis Edward, J.C.D., Excommunication, Its Nature, Historical Development and Effects, VIII-181 pp., 1928.
50. Reinmann, Rev. Gerald Joseph, O.M.C., J.C.D., The Third Order Secular of Saint Francis, 201 pp., 1928.
51. Schenk, Rev. Francis J., J.C.D., The Matrimonial Impediments of Mixed Religion and Disparity of Cult, XVI-318 pp., 1929.
52. Coady, Rev. John Joseph, S.T.D., J.U.D., A.M., The Appointment of Pastors, VIII-150 pp., 1929.
53. Kay, Rev. Thomas Henry, J.C.D., Competence in Matrimonial Procedure, VIII-164 pp., 1929.
54. Turner, Rev. Sidney Joseph, C.P., J.U.D., The Vow of Poverty, XLIX-217 pp., 1929.
55. Kearney, Rev. Raymond A., A.B., S.T.D., J.C.D., The Principles of Delegation, VII-149 pp., 1929.
56. Conran, Rev. Edward James, A.B., J.C.D., The Interdict, V-163 pp., 1930.
57. O'Neil, Rev. William H., J.C.D., Papal Rescripts of Favor, VII-218 pp., 1930.
58. Bastnagel, Rev. Clement Vincent, J.U.D., The Appointment of Parochial Adjutants and Assistants, XV-257 pp., 1930.
59. Ferry, Rev. William A., A.B., J.C.D., Stole Fees, V-135 pp., 1930.
60. Costello, Rev. John Michael, A.B., J.C.D., Domicile and Quasi-domicile, VII-201 pp., 1930.
61. Kremer, Rev. Michael Nicholas, A.B., S.T.B., J.C.D., Church Support in the United States, VI-1930.
62. Angulo, Rev. Luis, C.M., J.C.D., Legislation de la Iglesia sobre la intencion en la application de la Santa Misa, VII-104 pp., 1931.
63 Frey, Rev. Wolfgang Norbert, O.S.B., A.B., J.C.D., The Act of Religious Profession, VIII-174 pp., 1931.

64. Roberts, Rev. James Brendan, A.B., J.C.D., The Banns of Marriage, XIV-140 pp., 1931.
65. Ryder, Rev. Raymond Aloysius, A.B., J.C.D., Simony, IX-151 pp., 1931.
66. Campagna, Rev. Angelo, Ph.D., J.U.D., Il Vicario Generale del Vescovo, VII-205 pp., 1931.
67. Cox, Rev. Joseph Godfrey, A.B., J.C.D., The Administration of Seminaries, VI-124 pp., 1931.
68. Gregory, Rev. Donald J., J.U.D., The Pauline Privilege, XV-165 pp., 1931.
69. Donohue, Rev. John F., J.C.D., The Impediment of Crime, VII-110 pp., 1931.
70. Dooley, Rev. Eugene A., O.M.I., J.C.D., Church Law on Sacred Relics, IX-143 pp., 1931.
71. Orth, Rev. Raymond Clement, O.M.C., J.C.D., The Approbation of Religious Institutes, 171 pp., 1931.
72. Pernicone, Rev. Joseph M., A.B., J.C.D., The Ecclesiastical Prohibition of Books, XII-267 pp., 1932.
73. Clinton, Rev. Connell, A.B., J.C.D., The Paschal Precept, IX-108 pp., 1932.
74. Donnelly, Rev. Francis B., A.M., S.T.L., J.C.D., The Diocesan Synod, VIII-125 pp., 1932.
75. Torrente, Rev. Camilo, C.M.F., J.C.D., Las Processiones Sagradas, V-145 pp., 1932.
76. Murphy, Rev. Edwin J., C.PP.S., J.C.D., Suspension Ex Informata Conscientia, XI-122 pp., 1932.
77. Mackenzie, Rev. Eric F., A.M., S.T.L., J.C.D., The Delict of Heresy in Its Commission, Penalization, Absolution, VII-124 pp., 1932.
78. Lyons, Rev. Avitus E., S.T.B., J.C.D., The Collegiate Tribunal of First Instance, XI-147 pp., 1932.
79. Connolly, Rev. Thomas A., J.C.D., Appeals, XI-195 pp., 1932.
80. Sangmeister, Rev. Joseph V., A.B., J.C.D., Force and Fear as Precluding Matrimonial Consent, V-211 pp., 1932.
81. Jaeger, Rev. Leo A., A.B., J.C.D., The Administration of Vacant and Quasi-vacant Episcopal Sees in the United States, IX-229 pp., 1932.
82. Rimlinger, Rev. Herbert T., J.C.D., Error Invalidating Matrimonial Consent, VII-79 pp., 1932.
83. Barrett, Rev. John, D.M., S.S., J.C.D., A Comparative Study of the Third Plenary Council of Baltimore and the Code, IX-221 pp., 1932.
84. Carberry, Rev. John J., Ph.D., S.T.D., J.C.D., The Juridical Form of Marriage, X-177 pp., 1934.
85. Dolan, Rev. John L., A.B., J.C.D., The Defensor Vinculi, XII-157 pp., 1934.
86. Hannan, Rev. Jerome D., A.M., S.T.D., LL.B., J.C.D., The Canon Law of Wills, IX-517 pp., 1934.

87. Lemieux, Rev. Delisle A., A.M., J.C.D., The Sentence in Ecclesiastical Procedure, IX-131 pp., 1934.
88. O'Rourke, Rev. James J., A.B., J.C.D., Parish Registers, VII-109 pp., 1934.
89. Timlin, Rev. Bartholomew, O.F.M., A.M., J.C.D., Conditional Matrimonial Consent, X-381 pp., 1934.
90. Wahl, Rev. Francis X., A.B., J.C.D., The Matrimonial Impediments of Consanguinity and Affinity, VI-125 pp., 1934.
91. White, Rev. Robert J., A.B., LL.B., S.T.B., J.C.D., Canonical Ante-Nuptial Promises and the Civil Law, VI-152 pp., 1934.
92. Herrera, Rev. Antonio Parra, O.C.D., J.C.D., Legislation Ecclesiastica sobra el Ayuno y la Abstinencia, XI-191 pp., 1935.
93. Kennedy, Rev. Edwin J., J.C.D., The Special Matrimonial Process in Cases of Evident Nullity, X-165 pp., 1935.
94. Manning, Rev. John J., A.B., J.C.D., Presumption of Law in Matrimonial Procedure, XI-111 pp., 1935.
95. Moeder, Rev. John M., J.C.D., The Proper Bishop for Ordination and Dismissorial Letters, VII-135 pp., 1935.
96. O'Mara, Rev. William A., A.B., J.C.D., Canonical Causes for Matrimonial Dispensations, IX-155 pp., 1935.
97. Reilly, Rev. Peter, J.C.D., Residence of Pastors, IX-81 pp., 1935.
98. Smith, Rev. Mariner T., O.P., S.T.L., J.C.D., The Penal Law for Religious, VII-169 pp., 1935.
99. Whalen, Rev. Donald W., A.M., J.C.D., The Value of Testimonial Evidence in Matrimonial Procedure, XIII-297 pp., 1935.
100. Cleary, Rev. Joseph F., J.C.D., Canonical Limitations on the Alienation of Church Property, VIII-141 pp., 1936.
101. Glynn, Rev. John C., J.C.D., The Promoter of Justice, XX-337 pp., 1936.
102. Brennan, Rev. James H., S.S., A.M., S.T.B., J.C.D., The Simple Convalidation of Marriage, VI-135 pp., 1937.
103. Brunini, Rev. Joseph Bernard, J.C.D., The Clerical Obligations of Canons 139 and 142, X-121 pp., 1937.
104. Connor, Rev. Maurice, A.B., J.C.D., The Administrative Removal of Pastors, VIII-159 pp., 1937.
105. Guilfoyle, Rev. Merlin Joseph, J.C.D., Custom, XI-144 pp., 1937.
106. Hughes, Rev. James Austin, A.B., A.M., J.C.D., Witnesses in Criminal Trials of Clerics, IX-140 pp., 1937.
107. Jansen, Rev. Raymond J., A.B., S.T.L., J.C.D., Canonical Provisions for Catechetical Instruction, VII-153 pp., 1937.
108. Kealy, Rev. John James, A.B., J.C.D., The Introductory Libellus in Church Court Procedure, XI-121 pp., 1937.
109. McManus, Rev. James Edward, C.SS.R., J.C.D., The Administration of Temporal Goods in Religious Institutes, XVI-196 pp., 1937.
110. Moriarity, Rev. Eugene James, J.C.D., Oaths in Ecclesiastical Courts, X-115 pp., 1937.

111. Rainer, Rev. Eligius George, C.SS.R., J.C.D., Suspension of Clerics, XVII-249 pp., 1937.
112. Reilly, Rev. Thomas F., C.SS.R., J.C.D., Visitation of Religious, VI-195 pp., 1938.
113. Moriarty, Rev. Francis E., C.SS.R., J.C.D., The Extraordinary Absolution from Censures, XV-334 pp., 1938.
114. Connolly, Rev. Nicholas P., J.C.D., The Canonical Erection of Parishes, X-132 pp., 1938.
115. Donovan, Rev. James Joseph, J.C.D., The Pastor's Obligation in Prenuptial Investigation, XII-322 pp., 1938.
116. Harrigan, Rev. Robert J., M.A., S.T.B., J.C.D., The Radical Sanation of Invalid Marriages, VIII-208 pp., 1938.
117. Boffa, Rev. Conrad Humbert, J.C.D., Canonical Provisions for Catholic Schools, X-211 pp., 1939.
118. Parsons, Rev. Anscar John, O.M. Cap., J.C.D., Canonical Elections, XII-236 pp., 1939.
119. Reilly, Rev. Edward Michael, A.B., J.C.D., The General Norms of Dispensation, X-156 pp., 1939.
120. Ryan, Rev. Gerald Aloysius, A.B., J.C.D., Principles of Episcopal Jurisdiction, XII-172 pp., 1939.
121. Burton, Rev. Francis James, C.S.C., A.B., J.C.D., A Commentary on Canon 1125, X-222 pp., 1940.
122. Miaskiewicz, Rev. Francis Sigismund, J.C.D., Supplied Jurisdiction According to Canon 209, XII-340 pp., 1940.
123. Rice, Rev. Patrick William, A.B., J.C.D., Proof of Death in Prenuptial Investigation, VIII-156 pp., 1940.
124. Anglin, Rev. Thomas Francis, M.S., J.C.D., The Eucharistic Fast, VIII-183 pp., 1941.
125. Coleman, Rev. John Jerome, J.C.D., The Minister of Confirmation, VI-153 pp., 1941.
126. Downs, Rev. John Emmanuel, A.B., J.C.D., The Concept of Clerical Immunity, XI-163 pp., 1941.
127. Esswein, Rev. Anthony Albert, J.C.D., Extrajudicial Penal Powers of Ecclesiastical Superiors, X-144 pp., 1941.
128. Farrell, Rev. Benjamin Francis, M.A., S.T.L., J.C.D., The Rights and Duties of the Local Ordinary Regarding Congregations of Women Religious of Pontifical Approval, V-195 pp., 1941.
129. Feeney, Rev. Thomas John, A.B., S.T.L., J.C.D., Restitutio in Integrum, VI-169 pp., 1941.
130. Findlay, Rev. Stephen William, O.S.B., A.B., J.C.D., Canonical Norms Governing the Deposition and Degradation of Clerics, XVII-279 pp., 1941.
131. Goodwine, Rev. John, A.B., S.T.L., J.C.D., The Right of the Church to Acquire Property, VIII-119 pp., 1941.
132. Heston, Rev. Edward Louis, C.S.C., Ph.D., S.T.D., J.C.D., The Alienation of Church Property in the United States, XII-222 pp., 1941.

133. Hogan, Rev. James John, S.T.L., J.C.D., Judicial Advocates and Procurators, VIII-200 pp., 1941.
134. Kealy, Rev. Thomas M., A.B., Litt. B., J.C.D., Dowry of Women Religious, IX-152 pp., 1941.
135. Keene, Rev. Michael James, O.S.B., J.C.D., Religious Ordinaries and Canon 198, XI-164 pp., 1941.
136. Kerin, Rev. Charles A., S.S., M.A., S.T.B., J.C.D., The Privation of Christian Burial, XVI-279 pp., 1941.
137. Louis, Rev. William Francis, M.A., J.C.D., Diocesan Archives, X-109 pp., 1941.
138. McDevitt, Rev. Gilbert Joseph, A.B., J.C.D., Legitimacy and Legitimation, X-247 pp., 1941.
139. McDonough, Rev. Thomas Joseph, A.B., J.C.D., Apostolic Administrators, X-217 pp., 1941.
140. Meier, Rev. Carl Anthony, A.B., J.C.D., Penal Administrative Procedure Against Negligent Pastors, XI-240 pp., 1941.
141. Schmidt, Rev. John Rogg, A.B., J.C.D., The Principles of Authentic Interpretation in Canon 17 of the Code of Canon Law, XII-331 pp., 1941.
142. Slafkosky, Rev. Andrew Leonard, A.B., J.C.D., The Canonical Episcopal Visitation of the Diocese, X-197 pp., 1941.
143. Swoboda, Rev. Innocent Robert, O.F.M., J.C.D., Ignorance in Relation to the Imputability of Delicts, IX-271 pp., 1941.
144. Dubé, Rev. Arthur Joseph, A.B., J.C.D., The General Principles for the Reckoning of Time in Canon Law, VIII-299 pp., 1941.
145. McBride, Rev. James T., A.B., J.C.D., Incardination and Excardination of Seculars, XX-585 pp., 1941.
146. Król, Rev. John J., J.C.L., The Defendant in Contentious Trials.
147. Comyns, Rev. Joseph J., C.SS.R., J.C.L., The Papal and Episcopal Administration of Church Property.
148. Barry, Rev. Garrett Francis, O.M.I., J.C.L., Violation of the Cloister.
149. Bolduc, Rev. Gatien, C.S.V., A.B., S.T.L., J.C.L., Les études dans les religions cléricales.
150. Boyle, Rev. David John, M.A., J.C.L., The Juridic Effects of Moral Certitude on Pre-Nuptial Guarantees.
151. Canavan, Rev. Walter Joseph, M.A., Litt.D., J.C.L., Profession of Faith.
152. Desrochers, Rev. Bruno, A.B., Ph.L., S.T.B., J.C.L., Le Premier Concile Plénier de Québec et le Code de Droit Canonique.
153. Dillon, Rev. Robert Edward, A.B., J.C.L., Common Law Marriage.
154. Dodwell, Rev. Edward John, Ph.D., S.T.B., J.C.L., The Time and Place for the Celebration of Marriage.
155. Donnellan, Rev. Thomas Andrew, A.B., J.C.L., The Obligation of the Missa pro Populo.
156. Eltz, Rev. Louis Anthony, A.B., J.C.L., Co-operation in Crime.
157. Gass, Rev. Sylvester Francis, M.A., J.C.L., Ecclesiastical Pensions.

158. Guiniven, Rev. John Joseph, C.SS.R., J.C.L., The Precept of Hearing Mass on Sundays and Holy Days of Obligation.
159. Gulczynski, Rev. John Theophilus, J.C.L., The Desecration and Violation of Churches.
160. Hammill, Rev. John Leo, M.A., J.C.L., The Obligations of the Traveler According to Canon 14.
161. Haydt, Rev. John Joseph, A.B., J.C.L., Reserved Benefices.
162. Huser, Rev. Roger John, O.F.M., A.B., J.C.L., The Crime of Abortion in Canon Law.
163. Kearney, Rev. Francis Patrick, A.B., S.T.L., J.C.L., The Principles of Canon 1127.
164. Linahen, Rev. Leo James, S.T.L., J.C.L., De Absolutione Complicis in Peccato Turpi.
165. McCloskey, Rev. Joseph Aloysius, A.B., J.C.L., The Subject of Ecclesiastical Law according to Canon 12.
166. O'Neill, Rev. Francis Joseph, C.SS.R., J.C.L., The Dismissal of Religious in Temporary Vows.
167. Prince, Rev. John Edward, A.B., S.T.B., J.C.L., The Diocesan Chancellor.
168. Riesner, Rev. Albert Joseph, C.SS.R., J.C.L., Apostates and Fugitives from Religious Institutes.
169. Stenger, Rev. Joseph Bernard, J.C.L., The Mortgaging of Church Property.
170. Waldron, Rev. Joseph Francis, A.B., J.C.L., The Minister of Baptism.
171. Willett, Rev. Robert Albert, J.C.L., The Probative Value of Documents in Ecclesiastical Trials.
172. Woeber, Rev. Edward Martin, M.A., J.C.L., The Interpellations.

www.ingramcontent.com/pod-product-compliance
Lightning Source LLC
LaVergne TN
LVHW050207080826
844660LV00012B/370
9780813223605